Signs of a Happy Baby

Advance Praise

"I really enjoyed signing with my first baby very early on. When she was just four months old we started with the basics, and by around seven months she was signing back to me. Baby sign language made it so much easier to communicate with my daughter before she started speaking verbally, especially around meal time, and I really got to know my daughter's likes and dislikes, interests and ideas. *Signs of a Happy Baby* places everything you need to know about signing with your baby neatly in one place, including great tips, a comprehensive photo dictionary of signs, and lots of ideas on how to include baby sign language into your everyday routines. It's a great resource to have on hand and I'm looking forward to using it with my next child as well!"

—**Leah Busque**, Executive Chairwoman and Founder, TaskRabbit

"Being a new parent means you're anxious. You might fall more to the left or right of the anxiety continuum, but make no mistake – you're there. Learning infant sign language greatly helped ease my wife's and my anxiety as new parents – and it was fun! I was fortunate enough to take Bill White's class and started signing with my daughter, Haley, when she was about six months old. I taught my wife what I was learning (while she wisely chose to sleep in while I went to class). The benefit for us was we could much better understand what our daughter was communicating to us in very garbled sounds. Signed words such as 'all done' and 'pain' became immeasurably valuable. For that reason, I encourage all expectant and new parents to considering learning infant sign language. What Bill and Kathleen have created with this book provides a deep context for understanding why signing is so important to your infant. Additionally, they map out what to expect, when to expect it, and everything else in between with this new skill. Their personal story and advice are entertaining, fun to read, and very useful. Enjoy this book!"

—**Scott Brown**, MPH RD, Health Education Director
at Kaiser Permanente, Redwood City

"Baby sign language is, as my five-year-old would say, 'Magic, for real.' Not only is it the ultimate tantrum-tamer – via being able to communicate needs and wants prior to verbal ability catching up – it is also a tool for mindful, gentle discipline: less frustrated toddlers lead to less frustrated parents. It helps little ones share their fears and hurts, as well as what excites them, long before they can speak verbally. Harper and White have written an inspirational and helpful resource for parents to help them learn how to foster early communication with their children through baby sign language."

—**Sabrina Freidenfelds**, MPH, IBCLC, Founder of Then Comes Baby, a pregnancy and new parent resource center in Oakland, California

"Signing with a baby or toddler can open up your world in ways you've never imagined! It starts with simple, intuitive gestures and can progress to a complete additional language in your home. I highly recommend signing for anyone working with babies and children across the spectrum of developmental abilities and temperaments. This book is like having Bill and Kathleen as your private coaches – they will inspire you and help you easily incorporate signing into your everyday practices of parenting, teaching, caregiving, and nurturing your little one."

—**Dr. Tricia Tayama**, Pediatrician

"Brimming with tips and tools for getting started with baby sign language, *Signs of a Happy Baby* is a practical resource for any parent who wants to know what's going on in their baby's mind. Learning how to sign with your baby will create a wide-open window to what fascinates your baby, months and months before your baby will be able to tell you verbally. I've seen first-hand how Bill's baby sign language classes build parents' signing skills so they can better communicate with their babies, which deepens the bonds between parents and their children. Baby sign language is not only a fun activity for families but a valuable tool for children's language development. Bill and Kathleen's book is the perfect way to start."

—**Mora Oommen**, Executive Director, Blossom Birth Services in Palo Alto, California

"During workshops and classes, Bill's passion about baby sign language is clearly evident as he demonstrates signs and discusses the importance and benefits of signing with your child. Bill and Kathleen did a fantastic job translating that same energy and enthusiasm into this book; it is hard not to be inspired by their teachings! *Signs of a Happy Baby* is a wonderful resource that provides parents and caregivers important information about how to get started signing with your infant and provides a large vocabulary base complete with photos. Also, and maybe even more importantly, this book motivates you to get started right away by providing you with meaningful stories of the successes parents have had using baby sign language with their child. It's a must-read resource!"

—**Julie Dingmann**, Infant/Toddler
Program Coordinator, CCLC, Families@1st at Cisco

"Baby Sign Language is an instrumental tool in empowering babies and young children to communicate and express their needs and thoughts while they are pre-verbal and developing spoken language. Bill White is the paramount educator in his field and has brought deeper bonds, more attuned parenting, and *fun* to countless families, including mine. We are forever grateful for his work, both personally and within our community."

—**Ginny Colbert**, Education Director at Natural Resources, San Francisco

"*Signs of a Happy Baby* will convince you to start signing with your baby right away. The authors have written a smart guide that's not only fun, but filled with research showing how baby sign language helps build your child's language and cognitive skills, allowing your child's thoughts and feelings to be expressed, long before verbal communication is possible. This book is a must for anyone who has or is working with a little one."

—**Sheila Dukas-Janakos**, MPH, IBCLC,
Owner of Healthy Horizons Peninsula Breastfeeding Center

Signs of a
Happy Baby

*The Baby
Sign Language Book*

William Paul White and
Kathleen Ann Harper

NEW YORK

LONDON • NASHVILLE • MELBOURNE • VANCOUVER

Signs of a Happy Baby
The Baby Sign Language Book

Published in New York, New York, by Morgan James Publishing. Morgan James is a trademark of Morgan James, LLC. www.MorganJamesPublishing.com

The Morgan James Speakers Group can bring authors to your live event. For more information or to book an event visit The Morgan James Speakers Group at www.TheMorganJamesSpeakersGroup.com.

ISBN 978-1-68350-209-8 paperback
ISBN 978-1-68350-211-1 eBook
ISBN 978-1-68350-210-4 hardcover
Library of Congress Control Number: 2016914239

Cover Design by:
Heidi Miller

Editing: Grace Kerina

Author's photo courtesy of Christopher White, Photographer, littlebluemarblegallery.com

ASL Sign Language Dictionary photo credits:

Lenny Li, Photographer, lennyliphoto.com

Sabrina Wong, Photography Assistant and Post-Production Digital Artist, sabrinawongphoto.com

Courtney Laschkewitsch, ASL Consultant and Graphic Designer

ASL Alphabet and ASL Numbers charts courtesy of shutterstock.com

In an effort to support local communities, raise awareness and funds, Morgan James Publishing donates a percentage of all book sales for the life of each book to Habitat for Humanity Peninsula and Greater Williamsburg.

Get involved today! Visit
www.MorganJamesBuilds.com

Dedication

To the wonderful families who learned baby sign language in our programs.
And to our loving sons who inspired it all.

Table of Contents

Introduction

Parents learn baby sign language for a number of reasons: it's fun, they've heard it might help their baby get "ahead of the curve," and it might reduce frustration for the whole family. There are so many benefits for teaching sign language to your baby. The biggest reason we've heard from families over the last ten years might be true for you, too: you know there's a lot going on inside your baby's mind – and you want to be a part of it.

Children learn to communicate, whether it's in English, Spanish, Farsi, or American Sign Language (ASL), through receptive language experiences. Later, they acquire expressive language. This means that children understand words and concepts first and then later speak or sign to express their wishes, wants, and ideas.

Babies understand words as early as six months old. Spoken language begins when a baby is around a year old, with babbling sounds becoming words like "Mama" and "Dada," but it's not until the language burst at around 18 months, or later, that babies begin to express their thoughts and desires verbally.

Eighteen months is a long time to know what you want to say, have ideas you'd like to share, but to have minimal tools to express them to the people around you.

My wife, Kathleen, and I found out about baby sign language about a year before our first son was born. Kathleen was in a coffee shop, holding her fussy two-month-old nephew to give her sister a break, when a biker – in full Harley Davidson gear – strode up to Kathleen and told her she should be signing with her baby. A little taken aback, Kathleen asked him what he meant, because she hadn't heard of baby sign language, and he gruffly explained. "You use American Sign Language," he said, demonstrating with his leather-gloved hands, "so your baby can communicate sooner. It's practically criminal to not sign with your baby, because babies have so much to say before they can verbally speak."

A little more than a year later, our own child was born. Determined to be good parents, we bought Dr. William Sears' *The Baby Book*, Dr. Harvey Karp's *The Happiest Baby on the Block* book, the *What to Expect in the First Year* book, and a bookcase full of books for the baby, including *Brown Bear Brown Bear*, *Goodnight Moon*, Dr. Seuss books, and a few baby sign language board books.

Looking back, we didn't spend much time teaching our oldest son baby sign language in the early months. We did include the signing board book in rotation with the other ones. We signed *milk* and *more*, *cat* and *dog*, *ball* and *book*, but not much more. Our son seemed interested – somewhat amused, actually – but he didn't sign back to us.

One morning, when our son was about a year old, Kathleen and I were getting ready for the day while our son sat on the bathroom floor with some books and toys spread out around him. He picked up one of the baby sign language board books, opened it and looked at the picture of a baby with a hat on his head. Our son tapped his head, signing *hat*. He turned the page, looked at the pictures of balls in the book, and made a round shape with his hands, signing *ball*.

Our son was reading.

After that, we became sign language fanatics. I owned an ASL dictionary that had lived on my bedside table for a long time. Years before, I'd become interested in sign language after watching a Deaf couple sign across a noisy restaurant, easily communicating to each other while everyone else had to shout. As a dancer, I loved how physically expressive ASL is. And I had a degree in psychobiology (the study of behavior from a biological approach), so sign language appealed to my love of how the brain processes and learns language.

Kathleen and I started signing up a storm with our son and were quickly rewarded. Within two months, there were 40 signs he used regularly. We soon realized he was fascinated by anything that moved, like airplanes, pickup trucks, and backhoe loaders. He knew what he wanted to eat, what books he wanted us to read to him, and how he wanted to spend his time. In the six months between being one year old and 18 months of age, our son learned more than 120 signs.

I wondered why everyone wasn't signing with their babies. When I shared with other parents how my son was communicating with me using sign language, I was surprised by people's reactions:

"He'll never talk if you teach him how to sign."

"My daughter is going to talk soon enough."

"I know intuitively what my son needs."

"If she starts telling me what she wants, then I'm going to have to give it to her."

I felt sorry for those parents who didn't believe in the benefits of sign language, and even sorrier for their children. Children are wired to learn how to communicate in their first few years of life. Without sign language, the only other tools a preverbal baby has are pointing, grunting, and crying. Crying is an effective way to get a parent's attention, but not very effective in getting a baby what he or she wants. Parents have to rely on contextual clues to figure out what the baby wants and needs. In addition, according to many studies, crying is viewed as an "adverse event," which means parents are more likely to try to figure out what's wrong with a crying baby than to wonder, more specifically, "What's my baby trying to tell me?"

Sign language, on the other hand, engages children and parents and reduces frustrations for both. It gives children a way to start conversations and allows parents to connect, foster communication, and bond with their children.

I hadn't planned on becoming a baby sign language instructor or the owner of a business that has brought baby sign language classes to more than 13,000 parents, grandparents, and caregivers. For more than 25 years, I'd had a successful career as a commercial print model, primarily a hand model, with clients like The

Sharper Image, Allstate Insurance, and Apple. But when I realized I could help families communicate with their children long before babies were able to speak verbally, I knew I had to share my passion with the community.

The program I've been teaching for more than a decade to parents in the San Francisco Bay Area is based on American Sign Language (ASL). Many ASL signs are iconic representations of words, making them simple to learn and easy to remember. Some baby sign language teachers say to start with just a few signs and then add more as the baby starts signing back. My program is different. I like to call it "baby sign language on steroids." Just as children don't learn how to speak English or Mandarin or Spanish by being introduced to only a few words at a time until they master those, children don't learn ASL that way either. Babies' brains are wired to learn language; they can handle more than you can possibly imagine. Plus, depending on what age your baby is when you start signing with them, there will be a delay before your baby starts signing back. If you limit the number of signs you share with your child until they're signing back to you, you'll be missing out on the chance to introduce many more signs.

This book is a beginner's guide to teaching your child how to sign. Each chapter begins with a parent's signing story, to illustrate the many benefits of baby sign language. We'll teach you how to sign with your baby, citing research throughout so you're armed with information when you encounter skeptics, either in your family or out in the world. The book is filled with stories from families so you can see how signing has helped parents in many situations, from how a baby who wasn't yet talking helped his parents resolve an "ants in his pants" situation with his diaper (Chapter One) to how another set of parents discovered their daughter was a budding comedian (Chapter Five).

At the end of the book is our sign language dictionary, with photographs and descriptions of the signs you'll be introduced to in each of the chapters. We've also included charts for ASL numbers one through ten and for the ASL alphabet, which is used to fingerspell words. Signs are often "initialized," meaning the first letter of the word is used as part of the sign, so you'll see references to using the *B hand* or *G hand*, for example. In ASL, we use specific hand shapes, like the *claw hand*, to create many signs, so we've included photographs in the dictionary of those hand shapes, too.

Admittedly, it's harder to learn ASL from a book, because ASL signs often involve movement. ASL is a physical and visual language, and your ability to learn sign language from a book will be somewhat limited because it's hard to see the full movement of the signs in a photograph. To counter this limitation, we offer an introductory class that's available in our online learning center to help you learn and practice the signs. You can visit our website at happybabysignsclass. com to sign up for the class, which is free to readers of our book.

This book gives you a something other baby sign language books don't – a perspective on how to use sign language not only to foster early communication with your child, but to build your parenting skills. Each chapter ends with parenting advice from my wife, Kathleen. She's a certified life coach for moms, certified massage therapist specializing in pre- and postnatal massage, and an infant massage instructor, as well as the author of the Amazon bestselling book *The Well-Crafted Mom*.

What Kathleen and I discovered while integrating baby sign language into our family with our first son, and then later also with our second son, is that learning sign language helped us to become better parents. There's a correlation between how to teach a baby to sign and how to teach him or her anything: you pay attention, use your words, be patient, work through your own frustrations and expectations, and celebrate success (which includes whatever progress happens, no matter how small). As a parent coach, Kathleen provides support for moms by helping them discover what their children need and want – and how they, as moms, can keep from losing sight of their own needs and wants in the process.

Kathleen and I are excited to welcome you into the world of baby sign language. As you grow your signing vocabulary and teach signing to your child, you'll open a window into your child's world. You'll discover a special place filled with details about what delights, intrigues, and fascinates your baby.

Your life will never be the same.

Chapter One

Why Sign? The Benefits of Baby Sign Language

Signing Story: Signing Helps Your Child Tell You When Something is Wrong

"Emery had been signing *change* for about a month and a half, to tell us when he needed his diaper changed. When we were down in Southern California in the summer visiting my in-laws, he kept signing *change, change, change*! My husband, Brad, and I kept checking him, but his diaper wasn't wet, nor had he had a BM, so we kept saying, 'You aren't wet, you aren't poopy, you don't need to be changed right now.'

Well, Emery had a different idea about that, and he kept signing *change, change, change* for 15 to 20 minutes and began getting very upset, as if he was saying, 'Hello, Mom and Dad, I'm signing CHANGE ME!' Because Emery was so persistent, I said to my husband, 'Maybe something is bothering him. Perhaps the diaper is rubbing him or something.' So Brad went to change him and we were shocked! Inside Emery's diaper was an ant! A live, crawling around *ant*!

Well, long story short... my in-laws had a minor ant invasion upstairs in one of their bathrooms (the one we had stored Emery's diapers in). *Poor baby!* It was from that point on that we were true believers in the power of communication that baby signing can give a baby and his parents. Also, of course we felt horrible that we weren't trusting his signs before!"

– Crystal

Why Sign With Your Baby?

We all use gestures without thinking about it. You hold your index finger to your lips to imply "Keep quiet" and wave your hand to say "Bye-bye." You nod your head when you say "Yes," shake your head when you say "No," and turn your palms up when asking "What?" At a noisy bar, you signal your friend across the room and silently ask her if she wants a drink by pointing at her and tipping an imaginary glass to your lips. Babies use sign language when they lift their arms up to convey "Pick me up." They start imitating your gestures at a very early age when they shake their heads to say "No," blow kisses, and even bring a book to you to say, "Read this to me, please."

Signing is natural and unstoppable. When you sign with your baby, you take the natural human tendency to communicate with the whole body – not only with spoken words, but with facial expressions and body language – and give your child more resources to communicate what he or she wants to tell you, whether that's saying he has an ant in his diaper or she wants more applesauce.

Knowing what your child wants to tell you before he can use spoken words is a huge benefit of signing with your baby. Understanding your child's wants and needs helps you to know if your child is in pain, stop wondering what your child wants to eat, and discover why your child is crying, so you can do something about it.

"My daughter had her first ear infection at around 15 months old. She was cranky and we didn't know what was going on. She signed *pain* and then we took her to see the pediatrician, telling him that she signed *pain* at her ear. They found out that day that she had ear infection."

– Yunting

Signing is easy for parents to learn and then, in turn, to teach to their children. So many signs are iconic – they visually represent the word. For example, the sign for *baby* looks like cradling a baby in your arms, the sign for *milk* looks like you're milking a cow, and the sign for *cheese* looks like you're grating cheese.

In addition, the instructions for how to make signs often tell a story. Knowing the story often makes the sign easier to remember. For example, the sign *mommy* is made by tapping the thumb of your open hand on the chin because signs for females are made around the chin, signifying the strap of the bonnet that women wore back in the early 1800s, when Thomas Hopkins Gallaudet opened the first American school for the Deaf and the formation of ASL began. Male signs are signed around the forehead, representing a hat or cap, commonly worn by men and boys of that era. *Daddy* is signed by tapping the thumb of the open hand on the forehead.

There is an official ASL alphabet, and you'll probably guess at least half of that alphabet when you see it, because many hand shapes for the letters look like the written letters of the alphabet: the letter *W* is the first three fingers held upright, the letter *J* is the pinky finger swishing to mimic the shape of that letter, the letter *C* is the hand curved into a C-shape. Many signs are initialized, meaning that the first letter of the word is used to sign the word. For example, the letter *T* is wiggled to sign *toilet*. Take a look at the ASL alphabet chart in the dictionary section of the book to see how other signed letters look like the written alphabet.

"At 16 months, Charlotte has begun trying to sign the alphabet (especially to the tune of the ABC song). Now she recognizes the letters and constantly points them out as we go about our day (in advertisements, signs, markings, etc.). I know a lot of parents must think their kids are doing well and I really feel weird being one of those parents, but Charlotte definitely seems to be ahead of the curve. This is something we really attribute to the jump-start you gave us in speech processing at such an early age."

– Rick

Research studies have shown again and again that signing with your baby has a positive impact on brain development. Sign language utilizes more diverse areas of the brain for communication, thus babies actually develop spoken language skills earlier and have a comparatively larger verbal vocabulary than non-signing babies when they start speaking.

Signing empowers babies and gives them an increased feeling of control because they can communicate more successfully with those around them. Knowing Mommy and Daddy not only *hear* them but also *understand* them can provide a child with the feeling that her parents value what she has to say. This can lead to an increase in self-esteem, which can greatly contribute to a child's happiness.

Potential Benefits of Baby Sign Language

- Accelerates spoken language acquisition. Research studies have found that signing babies tend to speak earlier and have larger vocabularies when they do start vocalizing than non-signing babies.
- Provides a parent with the wonderful opportunity to open a window into their child's mind. By including signs in daily activities, parents spend less time guessing what children want and more time fulfilling their specific needs.
- Gives parents and children a way to establish a stronger emotional bond through one-on-one communication.
- Creates a fun activity for the entire family.
- Allows you to "discover" who your child is sooner by finding out what interests and excites her.
- Teaches a simple language that allows babies to easily express their immediate desires and needs, so parents don't have to play the guessing game, thus significantly lowering frustration levels for everyone.
- Creates two-way conversations by allowing a child to lead the dialogue about topics that interest him. When a parent then verbalizes the child's sign, it fortifies the baby's expanding vocabulary.

- Utilizes more diverse areas of the brain for communication. Rather than language being processed solely through auditory pathways, signing adds visual and kinesthetic emphasis to a child's auditory input.
- Gives babies a sense of control when they know those around them not only hear them but also understand them. This greatly enhances the child's self-esteem and emotional stability.
- Helps parents and health care providers localize pain and identify medical conditions.
- Enables children to express their fears and concerns.
- Decreases aggressive behavior – such as biting, hitting, and excessive noise – in preschool and elementary school programs.
- Increases a child's interest in reading.
- Builds an iconic bridge between two languages in a bilingual family. For example, the same signs can be used for words spoken in English or Spanish. Knowing a sign for a word helps a child recognize the same word spoken in other languages.
- Assists families with special needs circumstances by giving children a way to communicate if spoken language is a challenge.
- May actually improve a child's IQ. Research studies led by Linda Acredolo and Susan Goodwyn followed signing babies as they matured. At eight years old, children who had been taught signs as infants scored 12 points higher, on average, on IQ tests than a control group of eight-year-olds who hadn't signed. The signers had a mean IQ of 114 (75th percentile) versus the non-signers' mean score of 102 (53rd percentile).

Chapter One Quick Tip: Practice, Practice, Practice!

It might be a while before your baby starts signing back to you, so use this time to get comfortable with the signs you're learning by signing with your family and friends. It's really hard to remember the signs if they stay in your head and don't make their way out to your hands. It's like trying to learn a dance routine by only watching someone else do it.

If you're having trouble learning from the book, head over to our website happybabysignsclass.com and take our introductory workshop class. It's free for readers of this book. Seeing the signs animated on video will help you to practice, learn, and teach this great resource to your baby.

Kathleen's Coaching Corner

Imperfectly Perfect Parenting

"There's no way to be a perfect mother and a million ways to be a good one."
— Jill Churchill

When our first son was born, and even to a certain extent when his younger and temperamentally very different brother came along, I didn't feel like I knew what I was doing. I wanted to be the best mom. The perfect mom. Since motherhood was new to me, I did what I had always done when I didn't know what to do: I researched my little heart out. I purchased enough parenting books to fill a bookcase. I checked out even more books from the library. I went online and searched for answers. I subscribed to magazines and read them cover to cover, tearing out articles that answered questions I often hadn't even known I'd had. I asked questions of my girlfriends who had older children. I asked my sister and my mom. I asked questions of my sons' pediatrician (to his credit, he answered even the silliest questions with a perfectly straight face).

I had new questions every day. Is it okay to co-sleep? For how long? How do I know if I need to supplement breastfeeding with formula? What kind of formula? When do I start the baby on solid food? What baby food do I use? Do I make my own? Is it best to start with pureed fruit or with vegetables? Why won't my baby sleep? Why does he cry inconsolably every night between six and seven o'clock? Could he have colic? Isn't he too old for that? There's such a thing as swimming lessons for infants? Do we need to do that?

I had *so many* questions. And everybody had a different answer.

If *The Happiest Baby on the Block* book said one thing and my girlfriend with the really wonderfully behaved eight-and ten-year-old sons said something different, I didn't know what to do. I became so stressed trying to find the answers to all my questions. I ran myself ragged trying to figure out motherhood, trying to be a perfect mom.

Then I discovered the best advice. I kept a little book on my bedside table throughout the time my boys were little. At the end of the day, when everyone was finally asleep – at least for a little while – I'd read one of the short chapters. In the book, *Momma Zen*, Karen Maezen Miller, author, mother, and Zen priest, gently shared her stories of motherhood.

"Do not have any expectations about how things will go," wrote Miller. "Simply look, listen, wait, and trust. Then, just in time and right on schedule, you'll know for yourself."

I started trusting myself and tuning in to that inner wise me who knew that starting with sweet potatoes sounded like a really good idea, signing up for swimming lessons wasn't necessary unless we lived on a houseboat (we didn't), and I could trust that everything was going to be okay. Maybe a bit messy at times, but perfectly okay in the end.

Sign language helped to get me and the whole family to that place of trust. When my older son started using signs, he could tell me he wanted strawberries and juice and cereal for breakfast, please. When he started to get cranky, he could say he wanted to go to the park in his stroller. He could sign that his mouth hurt and, when I looked inside, I could see the jagged edges of a new tooth sprouting. He trusted me to listen, pay attention, and take care of his needs. I knew what he needed. I knew what to do. And I trusted myself more and more.

"Don't listen to anyone's advice. Listen to your baby," writes actress and neuroscientist Mayim Bialik. "We like to say, 'You don't need a book. Your baby is a book. Just pick it up and read it.'"

Chapter Two

When to Begin to Sign

Signing Story: Sign Language Opens a Window into Your Child's World

"Signing gave my husband and me a window into our little guy's mind that we wouldn't have otherwise gotten at such an early age. No lie, he woke up one morning at ten months old, and was slapping his leg like crazy. This continued a few mornings in a row until we figured it out. 'Are you signing *dog*?' Yes. Our kid was waking up thinking about dogs every morning. He was so excited that we understood him. And we learned that our kid's dog obsession was indeed real. So was his trash can obsession and his obsession with our neighbor, Bill. All goofy, and all things we'd never have fully understood without sign language."

– Ali

When to Start Signing

An optimal time to start signing with your baby is when he is six to eight months old. At this age, a child's long-term memory is developmentally ready to retain the words they hear and the signs they see. Babies also start developing the motor skills and hand-eye coordination to make more precise gestures at this time. After babies are six months old, they begin to associate language, whether spoken or signed, with the world around them.

A study published in the journal *Proceedings of the National Academy of Sciences* showed that babies as young as six months old could identify objects like an apple, a banana, and the location of the arm on a picture of a body. It's great news that babies are so cognizant of language at such an early age. The not so great news is that it's a long time after that until a child is ready to verbally communicate.

If you start signing regularly to babies when they're between six and seven months of age, you can reasonably expect them to sign back when they're between eight and ten months old. The timing of when your baby will sign back to you depends on many factors, like how often you sign with them, how well you put the sign in context so your child can make the link between the sign and the object. It depends on your baby's personal timeline. Every baby has their own agenda and, much like the timeline for when your child will take his first step or use the potty for the first time on his own, your baby ultimately decides when he is ready to start signing back to you.

It's perfectly fine to start introducing signs to your baby sooner than six or seven months. The sooner you start signing, the better teachers you'll be. You'll develop a solid signing vocabulary for when your baby is developmentally ready to start learning.

When my wife and I brought our second son home from the hospital, his older brother immediately leaned over the side of the bassinet and signed *milk*, eager to teach his little brother how to sign. Our younger son shared his first sign early – at seven months – probably because he had two adults and one determined big brother signing to him all the time.

If you begin signing with your child when she's older, she'll probably sign back more quickly. Older babies and toddlers are developmentally at that stage where they enjoy imitating Mommy and Daddy and they're already using gestures to communicate, like pointing to what they want and reaching their arms up to ask to be held. Don't be surprised if you see your older baby signing back to you within a week or so!

Whether you start signing early or later, your baby might use one sign for everything when she first starts to sign back. This is called *overextension* and it happens with sign language as well as spoken communication. Our younger son overextended the word *cheese*. He realized that when he made the sign for cheese, my wife and I rewarded him with smiles, conversation, and, yes, cheese. Lots of cheese.

"Like many kids, Brynn's first sign that she repeated back to us at ten months old was *milk*. We showed such excitement every time she signed it to us that she began signing *milk* all day, every day, with the hope of getting a positive reaction from us – not because she wanted milk."

– Colleen

How Speech is Processed in Your Baby's Brain

All speech, whether it is verbal or signed, is processed in the language center of the brain. Verbal speech is what we call *auditory*. When you say the word "milk," babies *hear* the word with their ears. That auditory stimulus travels from the ears to the language center of the brain to be stored as the word "milk."

However, when you sign the word *milk*, your baby is simultaneously also processing language in other parts of the brain. When babies watch their parents sign *milk* and hear them say the word, children hear what the word sounds like and also have the wonderful opportunity to see what the word *looks* like. This additional *visual* information travels from the eyes back to the occipital cortex, which is commonly called the *visual center* of the brain.

Not only does your baby learn what the word "milk" sounds like and looks like, your baby also knows what that word "milk" feels like. When babies start signing back using their hands, that is what is called *kinesthetic* information. The motion of their hands and arms is being controlled by a third part of the brain called the *motor cortex*. This part of the brain processes motion. Even though the motor cortex is in a distinctively different location than the occipital (visual) cortex and the auditory (hearing) cortex, all three parts have a multitude of connections.

Research has shown newborn babies have about 100 billion neurons (brain nerve cells) and about 2,500 synapses (brain cell connections) per neuron. By the age of two or three, a child will have about 15,000 synapses per neuron. For the first six years, a child's brain is busy hardwiring the circuitry for the mastery of complex language skills.

When babies learn language by passively listening to parents speak, they start to forge the connection between the auditory stimulus and the auditory cortex. This is necessary to process the words they hear. When you sign with your baby, she's building synaptic networks associated with speech not only in the auditory cortex but also in the visual and motor cortexes as well. Both the left and the right hemispheres of the brain are working together to process language.

Stages of Speech Development

Every child has his or her own unique agenda for meeting developmental milestones. Just as some babies learn to roll over earlier than others and some babies start to walk later than others, babies start to speak when they are ready.

Here is a timeline of how a typical child acquires verbal speech and how sign language fits into the picture:

0 to 6 weeks: Crying. Infants communicate verbally by crying. Crying is the only verbal skill they have to convey a message to the world that they are hungry, sleepy, uncomfortable, or in pain. Babies at this age become more calm when they hear your voice and often smile when spoken to. At this age, babies do not have control over their hands.

6 weeks to 4 months: Cooing vowel sounds and beginning hand-eye coordination. An infant's verbal motor skills are developing to the point that babies can start forming vowel sounds, such as "aaaa," "eeee," and "oooo." A baby may also vary his cry depending on his needs, like whether he's uncomfortable, hungry, or upset. At around three months old, a baby begins to slowly gain control of his hands.

4 months: Babbling consonant sounds and grasping. Motor skills are improving so that the tongue and lips can start producing more word-like sounds like "baa," "naa," and "taa." Your baby may also gurgle, laugh, and express her delight or unhappiness verbally. At this age, babies can grasp toys that are within reach and try to pull items closer.

6 to 11 months: Comprehension of words and greater motor control. Babies' memories are developing rapidly. They can begin to associate words with objects and actions. They often love to babble with adults, even taking a turn in the "conversation." Given the right motivation, they now have the motor skills to make hand gestures in order to communicate their needs. It is not uncommon at this age for some babies to start actively using their first signs, such as *milk* or *more*. It will be several months before they have the fine motor skills to make their lips, tongues, and mouth work in unison to form words.

12 to 13 months: First true words and even more signs. Around a year old, some babies have started to verbalize and say "Dada" or "Mama." At this age, babies' motor skills are sophisticated enough that they find it effective to use their hands to sign what they want.

12 to 18 months: Very slow verbal vocabulary growth but a big time for signing. Babies continue to comprehend far more than they can articulate in spoken and signed communication. A study of more than 1,800 children showed that children at 16 months of age can comprehend 92 to 321 words but can speak an average of only 40 words. This difference between receptive and expressive language can create incredible frustration for a child, which makes signing with your child so important.

16 to 20 months: Vocabulary spurt. There is a well-documented "vocabulary burst" that happens when a child has around 50 to 100 words. This word spurt can happen as early as 16 months of age or as late as well into the second year. Even though your child may begin talking up a storm, it's not always easy to understand what your child is saying. When your child's words are not clear, signing will greatly help you to know what your child is verbalizing.

20 months: First two-word sentence. Non-signing babies begin to put two words together, like "Mommy shoe" or "More apple." However, babies who sign have a larger expressive vocabulary than children who don't sign, so they will often start putting words together at a much earlier age.

> "Thank you again for introducing us to baby sign language. Orea, at 15 months, is doing more signs every day and it has been so much fun for us. Her most consistent signs have been *dog*, *bird*, *monkey*, *eat*, *milk*, *bath*, and *book*, and she even made up her own sign. She mixed the tilting of the hand for the sign *drink* with a thumb in her mouth for *sippy cup*. And every night before bedtime she makes sure she signs the word *book* several times so that we don't miss that very important bedtime step. My final bragging point is that Orea has been adding signs together to make sentences, like *more + milk* and *more + book*."
>
> – Patricia

What to Do about the Naysayers

It can be challenging to stick to your guns when people around you are unsupportive or even think you're ridiculous for teaching your child to sign. You may get criticism from your parents, your in-laws, maybe even your spouse. This can be frustrating, especially during the period when you're signing up a storm and your baby has yet to sign back.

When you're faced with a naysayer, remember why you decided to teach your child to sign. The benefits for signing with your baby, listed in Chapter One, include reducing frustration for both of you and accelerating spoken language acquisition, among others. You can also turn to the research that supports the benefits of teaching children to sign. Many studies are referenced in the Endnotes section of this book. When you know you're doing the right thing, you can trust your gut, politely ignore the naysayers, and keep signing.

> "We diligently began signing with our daughter and were met with a lack of response. My husband's parents and my parents reacted to our endeavors in different ways. Some showed a little interest but lost enthusiasm within a couple weeks, and some conveyed skepticism and said things like, 'She'll be talking before she signs.' Admittedly, after a couple months of not seeing

results, I lost steam and stopped signing. But almost the moment I stopped, our daughter came to the rescue and signed *more*. We regained our enthusiasm and haven't looked back since. Now, at 15 months, our daughter has demonstrated 28 signs, more than double the number of words she can say verbally. What's amusing is that I thought she would start telling me about things like diaper changes when she signed. Instead, she started by signing animals, like *frog*, months before she signed *change*. That's given us a look at what's important in her world – animals are huge! I now hear my once-skeptical in-laws proudly tell people about their grandchild's signing."

– Wendy

Chapter Two Quick Tip: Time it Right

Timing is everything when you're teaching your child how to sign. To help your child learn which signs go with which objects, activities, and words, make sure you always use the sign in context. Sign *change* when you're changing the baby's diaper. Sign *more* as you're giving your child more cereal. Sign *frog* as you point to a picture of a frog in her book. Create those associations for your child so that signing makes sense, and she'll start signing back very soon.

Kathleen's Coaching Corner

Making Magic in Your Family

"Temperament, you'll find, is highly dependent on time of day, weather, frequency of naps, and whether one has had enough to eat."
– Catherynne M. Valente

Sign language created a window into our children's worlds and, with it, Bill and I gained a better understanding of our children. Prior to becoming a mom, I believed that nurturing played a powerful role in a child's development and so, as a parent, I could strongly influence who my child became. However, 50 years of research reveals that in the game of nature versus nurture, it's a draw. In most cases, about 50 percent of who you become is based on your genetic makeup and 50 percent is based on your environment.

Temperamental traits – along with talent, intelligence, emotion, and a sense of humor – make up a person's personality. There are nine different temperamental traits, all of which are present in everyone to some degree or another. The nine different temperamental traits, as described by Jan Kristal, author of *The Temperament Perspective*, are: Sensory Threshold, Activity Level, Intensity, Rhythmicity, Adaptability, Mood, Approach/Withdrawal, Persistence, and Distractibility.

Each child comes into the world with a very distinct personality. When your child's personality is a good fit for yours, daily routines flow well: an introverted parent understands a quiet child, a busy family appreciates an active child, an unstructured mom blends well with an adaptable child. When there's compatibility with a child and his environment – and the people within it – it's called a "goodness of fit." When there isn't a match, like when an active child is with a more subdued caregiver, parenting can be more challenging.

Our first son tends to be flexible, optimistic, and mellow and has been that way since he was an infant, which worked well for Bill's and my ever-changing, self-employed schedules. When we kept our son up past his bedtime, he got sunnier, until he fell asleep happily on Bill's chest or in my arms. We could take him anywhere, and we did. He attended a formal wedding as an infant in a sling worn over my fancy dress like an accessory. We went on vacations and he slept in unfamiliar beds without disruption to his sleep schedule or routine. As first-time parents, we figured we were doing a great job of nurturing and raising our son. Our easy-going child was our reward.

Then our second son came along, and he had a different set of temperamental traits. From the beginning, he was more energetic and tenacious, and slower to warm up. We soon realized that our first son's easy-going personality had absolutely nothing to do with our parenting skills. As parents, we needed to develop new tools to support our second son, who cried more frequently and slept less soundly. We set schedules for nap times and bedtimes – and stuck to them – because our younger son thrived on a more regular schedule and became very upset when his routines were disrupted. Unlike his big brother, he wasn't easily distracted, so the parenting tricks that had worked so well to shift his brother out of a bad mood or bad behavior ("Look! A squirrel!") didn't have the same outcome. We needed to listen better to our younger son's cues.

The cues were readily apparent. Because we started signing earlier, our second son began signing back much sooner than his older brother had. By having a wide-open window into his world, we knew our second son's favorite foods and most-loved toys, so we could bypass a temper tantrum in the making. We knew what he liked to talk about, so we could direct conversations to the topics of trucks and trains when he started getting fussy. He could share what he wanted before his frustration grew too large and unwieldy for him to manage it on his own. Listening to our son and letting him "set the pace" allowed us to recognize his individual tendencies and temperament and to become better parents for him, which looked quite different from what being great parents looked like for his older brother.

"We know from myths and fairy tales that there are many different kinds of powers in this world. One child is given a light saber, another a wizard's education," writes Susan Cain, author of *Quiet: The Power of Introverts in a World That Can't Stop Talking*. One of my children thrives in an unstructured environment, the other requires consistency and predictability with his schedule. This is just one example of how my sons are so different from each other and how they need different support from me and Bill as parents.

Recognizing the best way to parent our children has sometimes been easy for us, but, many times, it's been hard work. The challenge is the same for you as a parent: to understand your child and discover how best to support her superpowers. Cain writes: "Don't just accept your child for who she is; treasure her for who she is."

That's how you create real magic for your family.

Chapter Three

Pay Attention

Signing Story: Signing Helps You to Develop a Stronger Connection

"Thank you so much for the gift of signing. It is really the gift of being able to communicate with our daughter. At 15 months, she has about 60 words (around 45 signs and 15 spoken words). Her range of communication – understanding and expression – is really wide. I am so grateful to be able to know what she wants to eat (usually pizza) and what she is thinking about (usually ducks). I'm glad to have this brilliant skill that helps us have so much fun getting to know Lilly through signs."

– Eugenie

Paying Attention Pays Off

Babies are programmed to learn language, and they learn best from interactions with you. Sign language encourages you to pay attention to your baby, and it creates many opportunities for you and your baby to engage in conversations. As early as six months old, babies respond to eye contact with their parents by smiling, cooing, and waving their arms. Infants follow the gazes of other people, and that shared point of reference is important for language and social development. Babbling babies even take turns in their "conversations" with parents by waiting until their parents pause before taking their turn to babble.

Sign language creates what researchers call "joint attention," which is when two people use gazes and gestures to bring their common focus to an object or activity. Just like language can be receptive or expressive, joint attention can be responsive or expressive. For example, when a child responds to an adult's bid for attention, that's receptive joint attention. Joint attention is expressive when it's initiated by the baby to direct a grown-up's focus. This process begins early and is built in to a baby's hardwiring.

Joint attention is an important part of language development. The more you can start conversations with your child by sharing a joint focus, the more you'll be able to teach your baby about the world around him. The more a child can direct your focus to what he's interested in talking and learning about – by pointing, looking, and signing – the more a child can communicate his needs, get you to talk about what he's interested in, and build his language skills.

A study by Brie Moore, Linda Acredolo, and Susan Goodwyn found that 19- and 24-month-old children who signed were more likely to engage in joint attention activities with their mothers than children who didn't know how to sign. Other studies showed that the more a parent and child engaged in joint attention interactions, the better a child was able to process information, control her behavior, and be well-behaved in social situations. These findings may explain why signing children speak sooner and have larger vocabularies than their non-signing counterparts, and even why there are differences in IQ test scores between signing and non-signing children.

You never know what your child is going to be interested in. Whether it's trucks or tigers, bears or balls, your child knows what fascinates her, and sign language gives her more opportunities to share her excitement with you. The conversations you'll have are not only fascinating and fun – they'll also encourage her language development.

———————

Here are some ways to connect with your child, engage in joint attention, and start signing and talking:

Pointing is a great place to start. Point to objects that are nearby, like food on the tray in her stroller, pictures in a book, favorite toys, and whatever else she seems interested in. When your baby points, it's important to respond to what you think your baby is trying to tell you. Pointing can communicate not only the object but the action; for example, when your baby points to an empty sippy cup, she might want more water. Don't worry that you might guess wrong. A research paper published in *Child Development* showed that babies keep pointing when an adult guesses wrong, trying to get the adult to respond correctly. However, the study also showed that when a grown-up repeatedly responded to the baby without enthusiasm, didn't talk about what the baby pointed to, or ignored the child's attempts to engage in conversation, the baby decreased her amount of pointing as time went on, essentially giving up on trying to communicate.

The lesson here is that when your baby points, get excited and show her that you really do want to know what she has to say. Say and sign the word for the object she's pointing to, and put it in context, like this: "That's your ball!" Sign *ball*. "Do you want to play with your ball?"

"Zinnia had been doing a gesture of pointing and tapping her index finger into the palm of her hand, and I knew she was trying to communicate something to me for a few days, but my guesses were all wrong. I thought maybe she wanted cheese or to wash her hands, but that wasn't right. It all became clear one evening in the kitchen as my mom and I were getting a rotisserie chicken ready for dinner. My daughter came up to me and repeated the same gesture and then pointed to the chicken. All of a sudden it clicked and I started shouting, 'Chicken! You want chicken!' My mom and I erupted in laughter and smiles upon seeing the joy on my daughter's face as she, finally, got through to us dumb adults. My mom was in such a state of awe as she remembered the frustrations she'd gone through with me in our early communications. The moment moved her to tears as she expressed her happiness that my daughter and I would have more tools to communicate at such an earlier age than she and I had."

– Carrie

Get on your child's level. Your baby will be more engaged with you if she can see your face and hands more easily. When you're at your child's level, you'll be better able to engage in joint attention activities, as well. Put your baby in a high chair so you're sitting face-to-face or, if she can sit up on her own, sit on the floor with her. Then you can sign and share with your child about the food on the tray, the toys on the floor, and whatever else strikes her fancy.

"My favorite part is the bond formed when signing. Babies are much more engaged when they know they have your full attention. You can't sign when you are typing on a laptop, iPhone, etc. Instead, we have to take the time to interact with our babies. I think babies realize this and appreciate it."

– Teri (baby sign language instructor)

Make conversation. Studies have shown that children learn language best from one-on-one interactions. Interestingly, research from the Institute of Learning and Brain Science at the University of Washington showed that children babbled more when a grown-up talked in baby talk. Baby talk, which is sometimes called *motherese* or *parentese*, is characterized by raised pitch and exaggerated pronunciation of vowels. This doesn't mean you need to speak to your baby with baby talk all the time, but speaking more slowly and changing your voice to emphasize the words you want your baby to notice can definitely encourage language development. Overall, the more you engage your baby in spoken and signed conversations, and the more opportunities you give your baby to babble and sign with you, the more you'll create a great environment for learning.

"I was at a coffee shop with my eight-month-old. I was carrying her while waiting in line to order. She kept doing the sign for *dog*. I had never seen her sign anything other than *milk*, but it really did look like she was signing *dog*. I said to her, 'Hmm, it looks like you're signing *dog* but we're inside a restaurant and there are no dogs allowed inside, but that does look like the dog sign. Do you miss our dogs? Do you like dogs?' She kept doing the sign over and over. I thought it was cute and kept chatting with her: 'Yes, you are doing the sign for *dog*. Are you thinking about our dogs?' I really was excited she was doing a new sign and was trying so hard to figure out what she was trying to tell me. Moments later, I turned around and saw that the person behind me had a tiny dog hidden in her purse. Yup! Dog!"

– Sharon

Chapter Three Quick Tip: Make Eye Contact

Making eye contact with your child helps build the bond between you, engages your child mentally, and gives your baby clues because he can better read your expressions.

Eye contact is also very important in language development. Scientists call it *gaze shifting* when your baby makes eye contact with you and then you both look at the same object. Gaze shifting is an early social skill that builds language skills.

Here's how to use gaze shifting to help your baby learn sign language: when you notice your baby making eye contact with you and then looking at another object, get her attention by making a comment, like, "Do you see the truck?" When your baby turns her gaze back to you, sign and verbally say *truck*. If the truck is a toy, take it to your child so she can play with it, and to make connections between the sign, the spoken word, and the object. If she's interested in a big truck outside, talk and sign to describe all the different qualities of the truck that you both can see.

Noticing what your child sees, making eye contact, and engaging your child in conversations – both spoken and signed – builds a strong foundation for your baby's language development.

Kathleen's Coaching Corner

You Can't Spoil a Baby

"The best way to make children good is to make them happy."
– Oscar Wilde

I'm a very nurturing person. It's no surprise, really, if you know me, that I was drawn to attachment parenting as a model for raising my children. Attachment parenting promotes co-sleeping, baby-wearing, and a focus on supporting the bond between parent and child. This parenting foundation suited Bill, me, and our children well. What surprised me, though, was how many opinions other people had about our parenting choices. It's amazing what perfect strangers would say to us. Perhaps even more amazing was the judgment from friends, colleagues, and even family members about how we were parenting our children. It was as if the baby in my arms broke down a social barrier and people felt more free to share beliefs, opinions, and what can sometimes only be described as utter nonsense. We heard statements like these:

- "If you respond to his every need, he'll never be able to do anything for himself."
- "Let him cry it out. He has to figure out soon enough that you can't be there all the time."
- "You'll spoil that baby by carrying him all the time."

On one hand, it seemed true that it would be easy to spoil my baby, especially because I was a responsive parent, maybe overly so. Back then, I worried about what people were saying and thought about backing off a little. Maybe I could encourage my baby to be more independent by creating as many opportunities as I could in which my son could be more self-sufficient. By letting him cry a bit longer before taking him out of his crib after his nap, maybe I could teach him how to play on his own so he wouldn't demand every ounce of my time and energy. Or maybe Bill and I should try cry-it-out techniques, since our son was old enough and Bill and I were so tired. Wouldn't that ensure our son wouldn't be spoiled?

It doesn't work that way. Research shows that the best way to build independence and self-sufficiency in later childhood is through connected and caring parenting in the beginning. Warm and responsive parents build happier, more moral, intelligent, and compassionate children, who then grow up to be happier, well-rounded, and secure adults. Children who have nurturing mothers have a larger hippocampus, the part of the brain involved in memory and stress management. Animal studies have shown that a mother's nurturing of a distressed baby alters neural circuitry in the part of the brain that processes emotions.

How the brain develops in infancy and childhood affects a person for a lifetime. Parents play a role in brain development through communication, conversation, and how they respond to the babies' cries.

In a seminal paper published in 1972, "Infant Crying and Maternal Responsiveness," researchers Silvia Bell and Mary Salter Ainsworth found a strong correlation between responsive parenting and the frequency and intensity of children's crying. Children whose parents responded promptly to their cries in the first few months cried less often and less intensely than the children of parents who didn't respond to cries quickly.

In addition, babies who cried less developed more varied and well-developed communication skills than babies whose parents responded less promptly. "Those babies who cry a great deal seem to lack other modes of communication," wrote Bell and Ainsworth. The researchers found that babies whose needs were met promptly cried less because they realized they didn't have to cry to get what they wanted. When babies cry less, they develop different ways to communicate what they want, leading to longer and more positive interactions with parents.

And that's the payoff: your parenting efforts in the early months help your child be more receptive to communicating in ways other than crying, like sign language. You create a model for your child of how she can ease her own frustrations in the future. When you ease your child's frustration by holding her and reassuring her when she cries; when you give her the words and signs to express herself; and when you act compassionately and lovingly when she's upset, you help her to build a stronger and more resilient brain that's ready to learn more and more.

I'm now able to see in my teen and tween sons the benefits of the commitments Bill and I made to them when they were young children. What often felt like exhaustion and what sometimes felt like sacrifice has led to two sons who are smart, funny, polite, happy, and a long list of other delightful adjectives. I remember my early worries about spoiling them and I'm glad I listened to my instincts about what felt right for me, for Bill, and for our family.

"Never fear spoiling children by making them too happy," wrote 18th century clergyman Thomas Bray. "Happiness is the atmosphere in which all good affections grow."

Chapter Four
Use Your Words

Signing Story: Signing Creates Conversations with Your Child

"I'm having a fabulous time with my son Marc, who still enjoys signing and is just beginning to mimic fingerspelling. One of my favorite moments (ever) was when Marc was around 16 months old. He put two books on the ground and started saying something excitedly that I couldn't understand. I then saw he was signing *train* in an exaggerated way, which helped me realize he was saying, 'Choo-choo.' I was confused, though, because neither of the books was a train book. As soon as I said, 'Train?' his excitement level soared because I'd understood what he was saying. He then pushed the two books together along the floor, showing me that he had *made* a train. He started adding book after book to make a longer train, delighted that I'd figured out what he was doing. It all started, though, because I saw that he was making a purposeful gesture that looked an awful lot like the sign for *train*. To this day, he loves trains, and I get to continue learning right alongside him about all different kinds of trains."

– Tricia

Conversations Matter

One day, when my oldest son was still a baby, Kathleen and I went to the grocery store together. We divided the shopping list to save time. She put our son in the shopping cart and headed off with him to start shopping at the produce section while I went to the other end of the store and began shopping. With my hands full, I found her in the cereal aisle and overheard her talking to the baby: "This is a box of cereal. It's the kind you like. See the picture of the cereal? Yum! The box is yellow, just like your shirt. See the color yellow on the box and on your shirt!" Our son was fascinated listening to her talk and began to talk back, jabbering baby talk whenever she paused and it was "his turn" to speak.

Conversations like these matter – a lot. Study after study has found that the number of words a child is exposed to in early childhood affects their language skills later on. Betty Hart and Todd R. Risley, authors of *Meaningful Differences in the Everyday Experience of Young American Children*, found that children are exposed to an average of 45 million words – words they hear and words they speak – by the time they're four years old. That number leaps to 70 million words for children in talkative families, and it falls to only 18 million for children in more taciturn families. At the age of three years old, children express themselves an average of 400 times per hour. Children from talkative families express themselves 600 times per hour, but for children from more quiet families, that number falls to less than 200 times per hour.

According to Hart and Risley, when children are with their parents, this is what they hear, on average:

- 1440 words per hour
- 90 questions per hour
- 17 affirmations per hour
- 7 prohibitions per hour

That's just the average, however. There's a big difference between what Hart and Risley refer to as "talkative" and "taciturn" parents. "Both talkative and taciturn parents use similar numbers of initiations, imperatives, and prohibitions per hour to govern their children," writes Risley. "While taciturn parents say little else, the talkative parents' 'extra' talk is mostly conversation about other things. The extra talk of talkative parents contains more of the varied vocabulary, complex ideas, subtle guidance, and positive reinforcement."

And that's what baby sign language encourages – the extra talk. Your child wants your attention and is eager to share what he's thinking. Using sign language with your child encourages you to engage your child, find out what interests and excites her, and to have conversations about all sorts of topics, which will then increase her language skills.

"I was so excited when Casey made her first signs. We were in Tahoe at a restaurant where a little girl had a ski helmet with a unicorn horn and a brightly colored mane on it, and Casey wanted to see it. The little girl was ignoring her, and Casey turned to me with a look of desperation and signed *hat*. It was the best thing ever."

– Dawn

To build your child's language skills and brain power, it's important to speak verbally when you sign. By combining talking and signing, you'll make the connections between the object or activity, the spoken word, and the sign. You can make these associations for your child in four different ways:

1. **Verbally label objects**. When you hand your child a ball, verbally label the object by saying "ball" and signing *ball*. It doesn't matter whether you sign the word before or after you point to or hand her the ball, just keep the timing close to the action. Babies learn verbal language by listening to what you're saying and observing how things play out. It's all about context. When daddy walks into the room, say and sign "Daddy" while pointing at Daddy. When you see a dog, say "dog" and sign *dog*.

2. **Create a verbal map.** An easy way to have a conversation with your child is to say a running dialogue of what you're doing, including whatever signs you know. Or you could describe with spoken words and signs what the baby is doing. By narrating what you and the baby

are doing, you're creating what's called a *verbal map*, which helps build your baby's vocabulary.

3. **Read to your baby**. Reading aloud is a great way to bring more words into your conversations while adding in signs. Signing with your hands full because you're holding a book is like talking with your mouth full: it's not ideal, but you still can be understood. If a sign requires two hands and you only have one free, the book can act as your non-dominant hand. If you have a squirmy child, you can prop the book up so you can sign better with both hands. Better yet, make reading a family activity and have your spouse hold the baby and read out loud while you sign along with it.

    The best books for signing have clear pictures of objects that you can associate with signs, like pictures of trains and airplanes, cats and unicorns, food and other familiar objects. Eric Carle's books, with their big, colorful pictures, are perfect for associating images with spoken words and signs. *Goodnight Moon*, by Margaret Wise Brown, is a classic and has detailed pictures of items you can sign.

    If you don't know the sign for a word while you're reading, skip over it, for now, (although your child may soon start asking you for more signs by looking and pointing at items in the book). If you're curious and want to learn more signs, make a point of looking up unfamiliar signs in the dictionary at the back of this book, in one of the sign language dictionaries listed at the end of this book, or by going to our online learning center, at happybabysignsclass.com and build your signing vocabulary by watching our videos.

4. **Engage in conversations with your baby.** When your baby babbles back to you when you ask her a question, or starts talking baby talk with you and then pauses as if she's waiting for you to answer, she's learning important patterns of conversation. When you engage in a "conversation" with your preverbal baby, you're not only sharing language with her, you're teaching her that talking encourages a response from another person. You're also introducing her to social

conventions of conversation, like listening, waiting for your turn to talk, and maintaining eye contact.

Hart and Risley make a strong case for having conversations with your child, with three key findings through their intensive research: 1) the variation between children's IQs and language abilities is linked to the volume of words parents speak to their children; 2) academic success for nine- and ten-year-olds is related to how much language they heard from birth to age three; and 3) children who are considered advanced academically have parents who talk a lot more to them than do the parents of children who aren't as advanced. Another study of more than 1,800 babies reinforced the link between talkative mothers and children with rich vocabularies.

"It's so wondrous when our daughter points something out to us, and it's fulfilling to have this two-way communication with her. She once signed *fish* while looking into a friend's backyard. I insisted there were no fish out there, but when I looked outside from her perspective, I saw that there was a rocking toy shaped like a fish! Another time, I was taking her home from my parents' house. As I put her into her car seat, she began crying. I started to try to soothe her, and then she signed *milk*. If she couldn't have told me what she wanted, I would have driven for 30 minutes with a hungry and upset baby in the back seat. Instead I took her back into the house, fed her, and then we had a calm drive home."

– Wendy

Chapter Four Quick Tip: Be Consistent

The best learning environment for your baby – for learning sign language or anything else – is one that's consistent. The more you can consistently make the hand shapes for the signs and associate the spoken words with the signs, the easier it's going to be for your baby to learn. Reading the same book again and again can be mind-numbing for you as a parent, but completely engaging for your child. Your baby might demand that you sing and sign the same songs over and over, and want to play the game of peekaboo repeatedly, delighted every time she sees your face appear from behind your hands. Consistency, clarity, and repetition is how your baby makes sense of her world.

"One day, Robert was extremely fussy. I was pulling everything out of my bag of tricks. He finally signed that he was sleepy. There I was shoving food at him, playing music, giving him a toy, and he just wanted to unplug and go to sleep."

– **Teri** (baby sign language instructor)

Kathleen's Coaching Corner

Sleeping Like a Baby

"People who say they sleep like a baby usually don't have one."
– Leo J. Burke

Bill and I didn't normally have routines, and that continued even after our first son was born. Sometimes we were up until late, other times we were in bed by 8:30. And that worked for us just fine. Because our first son was a go-with-the-flow kind of kid, it worked well for him, too. He could fall asleep anywhere. Baby number two was a different kind of animal altogether. He thrived on consistency, loved knowing what would come next, and liked to hear the same stories read over and over and the same music played again and again. We had to become more of a creatures-of-habit than a fly-by-night family.

"Infants love routines!" writes Harvey Karp, MD, in *The Happiest Baby Guide to Great Sleep*. "If you and your baby's other caregivers can stick reasonably close to a flexible timetable and regular routines, you'll all sleep better." What that means is sticking with the same schedule, even if the time varies a bit from day to day.

A study published in the journal *Sleep* looked at 405 mothers and their infants or toddlers with mild to moderate sleep problems. Half of the group made no changes to their nighttime routine; the other half introduced three activities as part of the child's bedtime routine. The activities were things like a bath; a massage for the infants, or the application of lotion for the toddlers; and quiet time activities, like snuggling or singing lullabies. The study showed that the children who were introduced to a specific bedtime routine fell asleep more easily, slept longer, and had fewer nighttime wakings compared to the control group with no changes to bedtime. The research found an additional, but not surprising bonus: the mothers whose children slept better had better moods overall.

A bedtime routine ideally should last about a half an hour and include the same three or four activities repeated in the same sequence every night. Pick and choose some ideas from the list below to build into your own routine:

Get your house ready for bedtime. If your child gets ramped up as bedtime approaches, you may want to consider changing the home environment about a half an hour before your child's bedtime routine begins. Dimming the lights and reducing everybody's activity and noise levels will create a calming atmosphere.

Give your baby a bath. A warm bath may help to calm and soothe your baby. However, if your baby gets excited or riled up when taking a bath, you might want to schedule the bath earlier in the day when it won't interfere with his bedtime routine.

Relax your baby with a massage. As a certified infant massage instructor, I recommend parents use pure oils like jojoba, sesame, or avocado for baby massage, to protect their children from harmful chemicals often found in lotions or other baby products. I also advise parents to avoid using nut oils until they're certain their child doesn't have a nut allergy, and to avoid introducing essential oils until after their baby is a year old. When your baby is older, you can add one drop of lavender or chamomile essential oil to the massage oil bottle, or even to the baby's bath, to help calm your baby – and to calm you, too.

Read to your baby. The sound of your voice is soothing to your child and can help relax her before bedtime. Plus, when you read to your baby, you're exposing your baby to the "extra talk" that Hart and Risley mentioned, and thus increasing the number of words she hears, which helps to build her vocabulary and language skills.

Play music or sing lullabies. Playing the same music every night at bedtime creates a cue for your child that bedtime is coming, and sets the stage for sleeping. Singing lullabies to your child also creates a soothing atmosphere. Your baby loves to hear your voice; he doesn't care whether you can hold a tune or not.

Use white noise. The best type of white noise for babies is low and rumbling, mimicking womb sounds. White noise can help to induce what Karp calls the *calming reflex*, that can soothe and reduce your child's nighttime wakings.

Cuddle with your child. Connecting physically with your child is soothing and helps him to feel safe. Studies of premature infants showed that babies who were cuddled had more predictable sleep patterns. Cuddling releases oxytocin, also called the *love hormone*, which reduces stress – not only in infants, but in older children and grown-ups, too.

When you're deciding which activities to include in your bedtime routine, take the time to understand what works best for you and your child and your family. Once you decide, do your best to stay consistent with that nighttime routine, including the time you start the routine, activities you include, and even the songs you sing for your child or the books you read. That way, your child can rely on those cues to help him go to sleep, thus giving everybody in your home much-needed rest.

As a parent, you teach your child how to fall asleep – and stay asleep – when you create consistency, encourage repetition, and model patience. This is a lifelong gift you give your child, a solid foundation from which to support her as she learns to communicate with sign language, roll over, walk, slide down a slide, swing on the monkey bars, play the piano, solve algebraic equations, and everything else she'll learn in her lifetime. It all begins now, often with a good night's sleep.

Chapter Five

Go Play

Signing Story: Playing Around with Baby Sign Language

"Our daughter, Asrai, started signing at nine months with *light*, followed by *milk*, *stripes*, and *dog* in the months following. At 12 months, she had around 25 signs. When she's trying to get something across that we don't understand right away, she will hold eye contact and try over and over until we get it or guess it. She signs to be read a book – *Read book, please* – sometimes with an identifying sign for different books. She signs for the food she wants and, of course, for milk, and delights in identifying animals, both stuffed animals and ones in real life. She also knows when to sign *please* to melt our hearts. Currently she is putting signs together to make short 'sentences,' most of which could be called jokes. Once, when she was asked what she wanted to eat, she signed that she wanted to eat her toy dog. She then put her hands on her face to signify *Oh no!* When I repeated back to her what she'd told me, she laughed hysterically and signed it again, until an appealing suggestion of a real food was made.

Another time she signed *cheese* while we were watching a movie and her father told her it was bed time, not cheese time. Five minutes later, she put her face in front of mine, saying and signing "Mama" until I asked her "What?" She then proceeded to sign *cheese time*. My husband and I just about died of laughter and I went and got her some cheese. The other thing she likes to sign is a noun + *scary*, like *Mama scary*, *baby scary*, *cheese scary*, along with rudimentary poop jokes – like when she laughs and signs *scary poop* after using her potty. In those cases, she's doing it for a laugh, but she also signs when she's genuinely scared of certain people or of cars, which is very helpful. ASL has given us more than basic communication. It gave us a little comedian!"

– Rayna

Signing and Play

If the greatest thing about baby sign language is that it gives you a window into your child's world because you get to understand what's going on inside of your baby's busy brain, the second best thing about baby sign language is that it's fun. Introducing baby sign language into your family is a great way to get to know one another and to enjoy playtimes using songs, games, and lots of other activities. Signing is easy to add to all the fun activities your family is already doing, like going on adventures to the park, dancing to lively music, and reading stories.

Here are more ideas for how to bring sign language into your family fun:

Explore and sign while taking walks. Getting outside is a great way to expand your child's signing vocabulary. You can sign all the things you see, from the trees and flowers to the barking dogs and the big trucks whizzing past.

When my older son was a little over a year old, we'd often take walks around our neighborhood. On one walk, he was fascinated by a neighbor's boat parked in the driveway. I signed *boat* to him and we verbally talked about the boat. Months passed before we walked that same route again, but when we did, he cupped his hands together and bounced them in front of his chest. My wife and I were initially confused, wondering what he was doing, and then it hit us – he had remembered the sign for boat!

Pretend by signing with toys and dolls. Symbolic play, also called dramatic play or make-believe, develops in the toddler years and helps children make sense of their world. Even if your child hasn't hit the toddler stage yet, it's not too early to engage your child in make-believe, like imagining you're listening to a beloved stuffed animal talk, and signing and saying a translation of what the animal is "saying." Or pretending a banana is a telephone and you're talking to Grandma, saying your part of the conversation as you sign the highlights.

Sing songs and sign. One of my son's early babysitters said singing is the best pacifier in the known universe. And she's right. Singing is one of the best ways to calm your baby. Your child doesn't care how well you sing or if you can carry a tune. She just wants to hear your voice.

"Research has shown that the sound of the mother's voice has the same effect on emotions as receiving a cuddle," wrote Sally Goddard Blythe, director of the Institute for Neuro-Physiological Psychology and author of *The Genius of Natural Childhood: Secrets of Thriving Children*. But the benefits of hearing the mother's (or father's) voice go much further. "Babies are particularly responsive when the music comes directly from the parent," continued Blythe.

In my baby sign language classes with parents and children, I teach many different songs that incorporate sign language. A favorite of many families is sung to the tune of "Frère Jacques." You can find photographs and written instructions for the signs for *walk, hop, run, stop* (and many others) in the dictionary at the end of this book.

Walking Walking
(to the "Frère Jacques" melody)
Walking, walking
Walking, walking
Hop, hop, hop
Running, running, running
Running, running, running
Now let's stop
Now let's stop

Another song parents in my classes love to sign is "Are You Sleeping?" which is also sung to the melody of "Frère Jacques." Have fun with this song, and add your own verses by switching the words "sleeping" and "eating" for other words, and using the signs for them, like *jumping, dancing, singing*, and even *pooping*!

Are You Sleeping
(to the "Frère Jacques" melody)
Are you sleeping, are you sleeping
Baby of mine, baby of mine?
Baby likes to sleep, baby likes to sleep
Sleep some more, sleep some more

Are you eating, are you eating
Baby of mine, baby of mine?
Baby likes to eat, baby likes to eat
Eat some more, eat some more.

No matter what your child's age, singing creates a great opportunity to teach your baby new information. When my son was three years old, I taught him how to spell his name in one afternoon by teaching him a song that put the nine letters of his name into a melody. When Kathleen came home from work that day, I led our youngest son into the room where he proudly – and so very sweetly – sang and spelled his name. Years later, our children learned (and Kathleen and I re-learned) the mathematical quadratic equation the same way – by learning a catchy tune that started with "x equals the opposite of b, plus or minus radical."

Play games. Make signing a part of games you play with your child. Playing games is a great way to interact with your child and give her opportunities to use her senses.

Here are three fun activities that don't require any supplies; just your eagerness and attention:

- Hide and Go Seek: Sign *where* and then the object or person.
- I Spy: Sign *I*, then *look*, then the object or person.
- What's that Sound?: Bring attention to sounds by signing *listen*.

Make sound effects. Sound effects will help you understand what your baby wants to tell you, even if you can't decipher what she's signing or saying. Your baby's fine motor control, which influences when she develops the ability to speak, takes longer to develop than her gross motor skills. However, your baby can make sound effects at a very young age. She can growl like a tiger, meow like a cat, even trumpet like an elephant, and these sound effects can help you interpret what your baby is trying to sign. Plus, it's really fun to hear your baby making playful sounds before she can verbally speak – and your silly sound effects as you play along will certainly get your baby's attention, too.

> "You were right, the added sound effects totally save us. I only know when she signs *balloon* because she makes a *ffftttt* sound like she's blowing up a balloon. Great tip!"
>
> – Rebecca

What came as a surprise to me as a father, and amazes many of the parents I work with, is that children are natural comedians. Like Asrai in the signing story at the beginning of this chapter, children are keen observers, eager to make us laugh, and will continue a specific sign or action if it's accompanied by a reward from you of eye contact, a comment, or – better yet – a big belly laugh.

One day, when my younger son was about a year old, I was changing his diaper (and his whole outfit, because it was that messy) and when I put his shirt on, both of his hands got caught in the sleeves, leaving several inches of fabric loose beyond his fingertips. He waved his hands a bit, watching the material move, and then caught my eye and clapped his hands together, making a barking sound. I laughed and he laughed with me. We both got the joke: *seal*!

Create surprises. A study published in the journal *Science* showed that children learn best from the unexpected. When faced with a surprise, children paid more attention.

"When my son Caleb was six months old, he was surprised to see balloons in my neighbor's apartment. Caleb was curious about them, so my husband and I signed *balloon*. Caleb didn't see that neighbor's door open for six more months. One day, their door opened and Caleb made the balloon sign, jumped, ran in circles, and made more balloon signs and sound effects. He remembered the balloons from when he was a tiny baby. I knew his little brain was capable and understood a lot, but that really showed how much he knew and understood at such an early age."

– Ali

Chapter Five Quick Tip: Put on a Happy Face, Sad Face, or Silly Face.

Sign language isn't only about using your hands; it's very expressive and incorporates your whole body, including your facial expressions. Facial expressions are a big part of how we communicate and figure out what's going on with other people.

Research with children has shown that babies take in a lot of information from other people's expressions. One study showed that babies will look longer at a picture of a happy baby versus an unhappy, frustrated one, signifying their interest in the more joyful baby. Other studies show that infants as young as a few days old can mimic grown-ups' expressions by sticking out their tongues or opening their mouths when the adults do.

When you sign, make your expression match what you want to tell your baby. When you're telling your baby about the trip to the park, give your baby a big smile to show you're excited. If you're sympathizing with your baby and signing *poor you* because he bonked his head, let your face also show your sadness. Expressing yourself with facial expressions helps your baby understand what you want him to know.

Kathleen's
Coaching Corner

Playful Parenting

"One thing I had learned from watching chimpanzees
with their infants is that having a child should be fun."
– Jane Goodall

There are many benefits of play for children. Play is how a baby learns about his world and himself and what he can do. Play makes children stronger and helps them learn new skills, like signing. Through play, children also learn social niceties, like sharing and cooperation.

Play benefits us all. Playfulness expert Lynn A. Barnett, an associate professor at the University of Illinois, has found in her research that adults who are more playful manage their stress better than their more serious counterparts. Being playful improves creativity, intrinsic motivation, job satisfaction, and even quality of life.

But it's challenging to find the time to play when you're busy being a parent, when there are so many chores to finish, and when you're so tired. Playing with your child can be delightful and engaging, but may not feed the creative part of you that's hungry for more.

Mihaly Csikszentmihalyi, psychologist and author of the book *Flow: The Psychology of Optimal Experience*, writes about how happiness is linked to experiencing flow. *Flow* is the sensation of being so engrossed in an activity that you lose all track of time. This often happens when we're playing. In your BC (before children) life, you may have found flow when creating art, writing, running, or working on a challenging but inspirational professional project. Now that children are here, in order to create a playful environment that encourages your own creativity, passion, curiosity, and flow, you need something that's often hard for a new parent to find: uninterrupted time.

If a neglected passion or a nearly forgotten hobby is tugging at your soul strings, look for ways to create playtime for yourself. You can trade "time off" with your spouse or enlist help with childcare from friends, family, or a trustworthy sitter. Another option is to use your child's nap time to focus on playing and finding flow, perhaps through craft projects, baking, or another at-home hobby.

If your BC hobbies no longer appeal to you, you can't find ways to make them fit into your schedule, or there's just no way you can enlist others to help with childcare, you can still create playtime for yourself. Ask yourself how you can combine parenting activities with what makes you happy. I call this concept *dual purpose parenting*. For example, putting the baby in a stroller and going for a walk with a beloved friend benefits both you and the baby. If you love crafting and art, unearth your supplies from the closet, put your baby in his high chair with "supplies" of his own, like vegetable-based finger paints or edible chalk, and play together.

Play is important. Play feeds your soul and gives you the strength to get through the rough patches of parenting. "Play is *exploration*," writes Stuart Brown in the book *Play*, "which means that you will be going places where you haven't been before."

When you play, you create stronger connections with friends and family, with your child, and, most importantly, with yourself. The more connected you are, the better you're able to communicate. Whether you're playing with your spouse on a date or with your daughter on the living room floor, everyone benefits. Go play.

Chapter Six

Watch This – Teachable Moments

Signing Story: Signing to Build a Tremendous Vocabulary

"Little Maddie is 16 months old now and, at last count, she was using 25 to 30 signs. Some words she signs exclusively – especially multi-syllable words like *elephant* – and others she both says and signs. There are a few words she doesn't sign often, but she will speak the words when she sees us sign them and will point out the object. Most terms, though, she says and signs interchangeably. According to her pediatrician, Maddie has a tremendous spoken vocabulary for her age – about 80 words now – and we attribute it all to the signing."

– Dori

Take Advantage of the Teachable Moments

Every day, events happen where you can teach your child something new. Teachers call these "teachable moments." Teachable moments are when you bring your child's attention to a situation in your environment to create a lasting

44

memory, demonstrate a new skill, or share a bit of your hard-earned wisdom. Teachable moments are fleeting, unplanned, and can happen at the park, the grocery store, in the bathroom, or at Grandma's house. The key point about teachable moments is they allow you to make a link between what's happening and what you want your child to know. Signing can bridge that gap between the moment and the meaning.

For example, at a crowded playground full of happy children, a toddler suddenly falls down, bonks his head, and starts to cry. Most parents watch with concerned expressions, but one parent says to her preverbal child, "Look, that baby fell down and is crying. He bonked his head," and signs, *Poor baby*. Weeks later, at the park again, that preverbal child runs over to his mom and points to a crying child on the other side of the playground. The signing child remembers and signs, *Baby crying. Poor baby.*

One day, when my son was a toddler and mostly still pre-verbal, he saw me take my mug out of the microwave after I had "cooked" the coffee for too long. The mug was hot and I drew my hand quickly away from the handle, hissing in a bit of pain. My son noticed my reaction: it was different, it surprised him, and he remembered. From then on, he was fascinated by my coffee mug: he'd reach for it, point at it, and sign *touch*.

One day, when my mug was slightly warm but not hot, I let him touch it. He drew his hand back in surprise and I signed *hot*, saying, "The coffee is hot." A few evenings later, when I was giving him his bath, my son stepped into the tub and immediately signed *hot*. I was surprised: I had tested the water before putting him in the bathtub and the temperature felt lukewarm to me, almost cool, not hot. I took my son out of the tub right away, added more cold water to the tub, put him back in, and he splashed around happily. Kathleen and I had always thought that our son didn't like baths because he fussed so much when one was imminent and then also throughout his bath time. What we discovered was that he liked the temperature cooler rather than warmer. My son's and my experiences with the word "hot" turned into teachable moments for both of us.

Throughout your day, look for opportunities to turn everyday events into learning experiences. For example, when you take your baby outside for a walk on a chilly morning, sign *cold* and say, with a shiver in your voice, "Brrr, it's cold outside!" Then start a conversation about how to get warm, maybe accompanied by both of you putting on coats and hats.

When you identify a problem and help your child figure out what to do next, you're not only filling the situation with the "extra talk" that Hart and Risley discovered is so necessary for language development, you're helping to build new pathways in your child's brain, creating an *if this, then that* situation she'll remember: *When it's cold outside, I put on my coat and a hat.*

To teach your child to sign, use learning opportunities in your day-to-day activities. Children learn sign language best in an immersive environment, just like they learn spoken language by being immersed in hearing it all the time. The best way to build your child's spoken and signed vocabulary is to talk and sign as much as you can throughout the day. When you're feeding your baby, sign the foods that you're offering, like *cereal* and *strawberry*. When you play, sign the names of the toys, like *bear* for your daughter's beloved stuffed bear. When you're outside, sign *tree* when your daughter touches the tree, sign *swing* when you put her in the swing, sign *dog* when you see the dog. You can't overload your baby's brain; she's hungry for lots of information, and there's room for it all.

It's easy to teach your child the signs for physical objects in her world, but how do you teach abstract concepts like *hot*, *cold*, *yes*, and *no*? It can be a little more challenging to connect these types of words with signs.

Here's what you can do to teach your child how to sign *more*: Put one slice of banana on her tray. After she eats the piece and makes eye contact with you, say, "Would you like more?" sign *more*, and give her more banana. When your child consistently receives more as you sign *more*, she'll quickly grasp the concept. In fact, *more* is typically one of the first signs a child uses.

When you're teaching the concepts of *yes* and *no*, make sure your facial expressions and behaviors match your words, so your child learns from your body language, too. Combine saying "yes" with nodding your head, signing *yes*, and smiles and praise. Combine the verbal command "no" with shaking your head, signing *no*, looking stern, and removing the child from the tempting situation, like when he wants to put sand in his mouth at the playground. Putting the word into context is key for teaching abstract concepts.

"I was surprised by how much my daughter could express at such a young age. It wasn't just concrete things, like food and milk, but abstract ideas, too. I really got to see her imagination at work. I remember giving her prune Jell-O one day. When a small piece fell, making an arc on her highchair tray, she pointed to it and signed *rainbow*. I was very impressed!"

– Aubri

Bridging the Gap in a Bilingual Family

When a baby is raised in a bilingual family, sign language is what we call the *bilingual bridge*. It creates a strong connection between the two verbal languages. If there are people in your child's life, like grandparents and caregivers, who speak a different language, or if you want to expose your child to two or more languages, signing can really help, because the same sign can be used for the same word spoken in different languages. Whether you're speaking Japanese, English, Spanish, or any other spoken language, signing is like having closed captioning wherever you go.

"As my daughter started to talk, she used the sign and said the spoken word in English or Spanish, whichever one was the simplest for her to pronounce. If I asked her in Spanish to pick up her "zapatos" as I used the sign for *shoes*, she would sign *shoes* but would verbally say "shoes," in English, because it was easier for her to pronounce than "zapatos." The same thing happened with other words, like *ball/pelota* or *bird/pajaro*. Signing was a bridge between our spoken language at home (Spanish) and the language of the outside world (English). That's how she gained vocabulary in both languages simultaneously."

– Chantal

If you and your spouse are using the OPOL (one parent, one language) approach of one of you speaking English to the child and the other speaking another language, you'll both use the same signs but will speak the words for the sign that are specific to the different languages. For example, when you're feeding your child, you say, "This is milk," and sign *milk*. When your spouse feeds the baby, he says "Esto es la leche," and gives the same sign you did. The consistent sign – in this case *milk* – will give your baby the information he needs to make the connections between all three languages – English, Spanish, and ASL.

"My parents speak Spanish, my in-laws speak Hindi, and my husband and I speak English at home. Because of signing, my daughter didn't have to cry for what she needed. She got really good about telling us if she was sleepy, needed a diaper change, or wanted milk or food. And we all understood what she needed."

– Julieta

Chapter Six Quick Tip: Dominant and Non-Dominant Hands

When using sign language, you choose one hand as your dominant hand. Typically, the hand you write with is your dominant hand. Your other hand is the non-dominant hand. If you're left-handed, like my wife, it's okay to use your left hand as your dominant hand. The most important thing to remember is to not go back and forth between which hand you use as your dominant hand. If you keep switching the hand you use as dominant, it will be harder for others to understand what you're signing.

When you sign, your hands can move in one of three different patterns:

1. Only your dominant hand moves, like when you sign *yes*, *no*, *sleep*, or *eat*. If you're holding something – like your baby – with your dominant hand, it's perfectly fine to sign with your non-dominant hand.
2. Your dominant and non-dominant hands move together in the same positions, like when you sign *cold*, *cat*, or *all done*.
3. Your dominant hand moves while the non-dominant hand stays stationary, but is needed to do the sign, like for the signs *night*, *jump*, or *whale*. In this situation, your non-dominant hand acts as the environment – the horizon, the ground, or the surface of the sea – and stays stable. If you don't have two free hands to sign, try using whatever you're holding

as the non-dominant hand, like using the book you're carrying for the ground as you sign *jump*.

Check out the dictionary later on in the book to see photographs and read descriptions of how to make many of the signs we mention in the book. Or go to happybabysignsclass.com to sign up for your free introductory class to help you practice and learn more signs to teach to your child.

Kathleen's Coaching Corner

Learning the Hard Way (for You)

"The hardest part of raising a child is teaching them to ride bicycles. A shaky child on a bicycle for the first time needs both support and freedom. The realization that this is what the child will always need can hit hard."
– Sloan Wilson

It's so tempting. Your baby is just a few inches shy of rolling over completely. Just a little nudge and he'd be all the way on his tummy. Or he's reaching and reaching for the toy that's just out of his grasp. Or he's older now and wants to get to the top of the play structure but can't manage the ladder yet. Do you help? Do you give your son a gentle push to help him roll over, scoot the toy closer, or lift him to the top of the slide?

The answer is a resounding … *maybe*.

Maybe yes, because a frustrated child's full-blown meltdown isn't good for anyone's well-being. Or maybe no, because struggle is a key part of the learning process – your child needs to feel stuck and frustrated sometimes.

Children learn best when they accomplish a feat all on their own, without parental nudges or help. Just as a child's brain is wired to learn, her body is programmed to explore. Your baby bangs, bangs, bangs her feet on the side of the crib, watches the colorful mobile swing above her head, and makes the connection between her actions and the outcome. She tries to roll but her arm is in the way. She tries to roll again but still can't get over. She tries again and again, each time making small changes to her position until she finally rolls all the way over onto her tummy, exactly where she wants to be (until she decides she wants to lie on her back and can't figure out how to roll back over).

Allowing your child to make mistakes, struggle, and deal with frustration can be hard for you as a parent. When your child learns on his own, however, he builds resilience, confidence, and problem-solving skills.

Here are four ways to step back and let your child learn on his own:

Wait a minute. I always thought that a good mom was one who was intensely responsive to her child. I discovered, however, that when I rushed to the rescue, my child began to count on me to save him: to find his pacifier lost somewhere in the crib, to get the toy that had rolled out of his reach, to carry him from the boring place where he was to the more exciting place where he wanted to be.

There's a delicate line between your child's "good" frustration and "bad" frustration and you can hear it in his voice and how he cries. If your child is fussing but not howling, try to stay in that middle place between going to the rescue and letting your child figure it out. Waiting just a minute can make a big difference in how confident your child becomes about learning on his own.

Create a verbal map. In Chapter Four, Bill recommended using verbal maps to build a child's vocabulary by describing what's happening in the child's environment. Verbal maps can also be very helpful for walking a child through learning a new skill. Creating a verbal map for a child who is struggling with being stuck might sound like this: "Oh, I see you're standing up. Did you pull yourself up and now can't get down again? That's a problem, isn't it? Can you sit down by holding on to the edge of your crib and then dropping your bottom?"

Acknowledge her frustration. Giving words to what your child may be feeling is a wonderful way to encourage her emotional and social development. You can even include signs like *frustrated* and *angry* as she tries to learn a new skill, and *happy* and *excited* when she makes progress. Just hearing your voice can help to ease her frustration, too.

Step in with love when needed. When good frustration turns into bad frustration and your child becomes overwhelmed from trying, you have a few options of what to do. You could distract your child with another activity to give your child time to calm down before trying the challenging task again. You could help your child by assisting him with the next baby step of the process, like showing him how to move his foot up to the next step on the ladder to the slide. You could motivate your child to keep trying, perhaps by offering him what he loves the most.

What our older son loved the most when he was a baby was O-shaped cereal. At ten months old, he wasn't crawling yet. Bill and I, as new parents, were a bit concerned that he hadn't met this developmental milestone. One afternoon, we removed our son's socks and pants so his bare feet and legs would have the most traction, and we made a trail of cereal on the floor. We put our son on the floor and sat back to watch and wait on the sidelines while he learned to crawl, lured by what he loved.

The sidelines was a place that would become very familiar for us as parents of our first son: the floor of our family room when he learned to crawl, the hard seats in the elementary school auditorium when he took to the stage for the first time, our folding chairs on the field when he played soccer, the theater seats when he performed in the band. He played, performed, or practiced while we sat on the sidelines, trying our best to get comfortable in that precious place between offering support and setting him free.

I remember the day our son learned to crawl as one of many where Bill and I looked for the best balance between stepping in to support and stepping back to let him learn on his own, searching for the teachable moments for us all.

Chapter Seven

You're Okay – Patience and Positivity

Signing Story: Signing Provides Relief from Whining

"At 15 months old, our daughter Sienna is signing about 20 different signs – some helpful, some just cute! I especially love when she signs *please*, *thank you*, *beautiful*, and *red*. What we find most helpful is that when Sienna is whining for something, we can say to her, 'Please use your signs,' and she will stop whining and try to tell us what she wants us to know. This is a relief from the whining but, more importantly, she can tell us something and she can understand us. We can't believe that she really gets things this early in her life – much more than we'd thought."

– Koryn

Signing Helps Ease Everybody's Frustration

Being a baby can be frustrating. Your baby doesn't have control over his physical body. He doesn't have control over his environment, like being able to get what he wants to eat when he's hungry. And he can't communicate very well with the people around him. Sure, he can cry when he's frustrated, tired, hungry, or uncomfortable, but crying doesn't always get him what he wants. Sometimes he cries when he doesn't want to be in the swing anymore but then is offered milk instead of taken out of the swing – and he's not hungry. Or he cries because he's hungry, but gets put in the swing instead of being given something to eat, and that makes him cry even more.

Being a parent can be just as frustrating. Your baby cries for no apparent reason, pushes away your offer of milk or his pacifier, and gets more and more upset with all of your attempts to soothe him. Again and again, you find yourself wondering what he wants and what you can do to get him to stop crying.

Teaching your baby how to sign will mean he'll be able to use signs to tell you if he wants more cereal or wants to get down from his high chair – but it won't happen right away. In the beginning, when you're teaching your child to sign, there will probably be a gap of time between introducing signs and your baby starting to sign back. This delay can lead to even more frustration for everyone for a while.

The amount of time you'll have to wait for your child to start signing back is unpredictable. It might feel like you're signing and signing at your child and all of your gestures and good intentions are going into a void. It's important, however, to be patient while you wait for your baby to develop her expressive language skills so she can communicate with signs (and, later, verbally). Trust me: the information is all going in. Your child is learning far more words and signs through receptive language than you probably realize.

"Months ago, we stopped doing signs for a while because our daughter didn't seem to be learning them. But then she surprised us by signing tons, and we had to work hard to remember our signs so we could know what she was trying to tell us."
— Sharon

What can also be frustrating is that there's a wide timeline for when it's typical for babies to start talking or signing. You might look around and see other babies, younger than your own, who are already signing. When your baby will reach those expressive language milestones depends on so many factors, like your baby's individual timeline for physical development, for example, and how often and how consistently you're signing to your baby.

What's known for certain is that signing will not delay your baby's verbal communication but will, in fact, enhance it. Research by Linda Acredolo and Susan Goodwyn, child development experts who founded the baby sign language movement, discovered that children whose parents taught them symbolic gesturing (baby signs) had greater vocabularies than children whose parents were not trained to use signs or who were asked to use only spoken words while communicating with their children.

A study published in the *Journal of Speech, Language, and Hearing Research* looked at verbally delayed children and found that the number of gestures these "late talkers" used indicated their later language abilities. Late talkers who used more gestures to communicate were more likely to catch up with their more verbal peers.

> "My son was speech-delayed. I knew he was intelligent. He didn't say 'Mama' until he was 18 months old, but he was never frustrated, because he was able to sign what he needed. He's seven years old now and in second grade. He is articulate, his vocabulary is advanced, and he is reading at a sixth grade level."
>
> **– Camie**

While you're waiting for your child to meet a developmental milestone, whether it's signing or verbally speaking her first word, crawling, or going poop in the potty, it's important to stay positive. I tell parents in my workshops to praise their children's efforts when they're learning something new. If your child is potty training and poops next to the potty, say "That's great! You pooped *near* your potty! Next time, you'll get even closer." When your child is learning to sign and makes a mistake when she signs a word – like pointing her index finger to the palm of her other hand to sign *more* (an error babies frequently make when learning to sign) instead of tapping the fingertips and thumbs of both hands together – acknowledge what she is signing by saying the word "more" out loud, and then simply sign the word back to her correctly while asking, "Do you want more?"

A study published in *Infant Behavior and Development* showed that parents and their children were less frustrated when they used signs to communicate. Another study demonstrated that when parents were warm, caring, and positive, their children were better able to regulate their emotions and were less angry, frustrated, and aggressive. Signing and positive parenting work well together to help children develop language skills, social skills, and emotional regulation.

> "Sign language has prevented a lot of frustration in our home. Because Cora can communicate her wants and needs with us, she tends to not get upset and frustrated so quickly."
>
> – Robin

Especially during the early years, there's a big emphasis on meeting the milestones, and it can be disappointing when your child's development looks different from what's average. A good parenting skill to start practicing now is to acknowledge your child's progress and all of her efforts, not only the outcomes. Research shows that children who are praised not just for the results, but for their efforts – for example, by saying things like, "You're trying really hard to tell me what you want" – are more likely to be persistent and have good self-esteem, whether or not they succeed at the task at hand. Just like at a baseball game when a child at home plate swings and totally misses the ball and parents and coaches yell, "Good swing!" the right kind of praise rewards the effort at bat, not just the base hit.

Carol Dweck, Stanford psychologist and author of *Mindset: How You Can Fulfill Your Potential*, found in her research that kids who receive praise for their efforts are more resilient and eager to be challenged. These kids also believe that their intelligence isn't set in stone and that hard work can make them smarter. On the other hand, kids who are praised for their personal qualities are less motivated and more uncomfortable with taking risks, because they're afraid they might fail.

When your baby is signing to you, praising her efforts might sound like: "Good signing! You're using your hands to tell me what you want." Or, when she's verbally babbling, you can sound very interested and say, "Really! Tell me the rest of the story."

Even when your child is young, your encouragement of her efforts matters a great deal. A study published in *Child Development* showed that two-year-olds whose mothers encouraged their independence and praised their efforts while the child was attempting a difficult task were more likely to become three-year-olds who persistently tackled challenges.

> "It's been so nice to use baby sign language with my daughter when she's making sounds of frustration. I can remind her to use her hands to indicate if she's *all done* or wants *more*."
>
> – Shannon

Chapter Seven Quick Tip: Hand-on-Hand Learning

One of the best ways to teach your child a physical skill like sign language is to guide their hands. In my family, we call it *hand-on-hand learning*.

When my sons were small and learning to use crayons, I'd gently wrap my hands around theirs and guide their hands to help them get the feel of the crayon they were holding, then let go once they started to get the hang of it. Later, I did hand-on-hand learning to teach my older son how to swing a baseball bat. But the first times I used hand-on-hand learning were to teach my older son to sign, by moving his hand in a circle on his chest to sign *please*, lifting his finger and waggling it back and forth to sign *where* when he was seeking the teddy bear I had hidden in his room during a game of hide-and-go-seek, and holding his wrist and wiggling his hand to sign *blue*.

You can do the same thing to help your child learn to sign. If your child will let you, touch-guide her hands to create the shapes of the signs. If your child pulls away, don't force her, just look for another time when you can try hand-on-hand learning again. The trick to being a good teacher to your child is knowing the best timing for getting your message across. Learn to listen not only with your ears but also with your eyes, mind, and heart to notice when she's receptive to learning.

"We waited and kept signing and then, all of a sudden, when our daughter was between 12 and 14 months old, her signing really exploded. It was like Lily looked at her fingers and suddenly figured out 'I can tell them what I want with these things!' By 16 months she was making about 60 to 70 different signs. It helped that Pete and I each taught and used different signs with her, so she had a larger vocabulary than either of us did. Lily is now 20 months and speaking very clearly and has a large verbal vocabulary. She picks up and knows words the first time she hears them. She still uses signs a lot, too. She always signs and says 'please' at the same time. Her grandparents cannot stop telling people about it. They think it is so cool."

– Ginger

Kathleen's Coaching Corner

Finding Patience for Yourself

"You can learn so many things from children.
How much patience you have, for instance."
– Franklin P. Adams

The combination of sleep deprivation and a crying baby can create a concoction of frustration, disappointment, stress, and even anger for new parents. When your brain is deprived of sleep, your prefrontal cortex doesn't work so well. It's as if your brain's chief executive officer has been demoted to the mail room, making it really hard to make decisions, keep your patience, and even remember the smallest of tasks. It's easy to lose your keys and your temper, because both memory and willpower require brain power, which you don't have when you're sleep deprived. It's a conundrum: having the patience to deal with your baby's cries takes brain power that you don't have because you've been awake so long dealing with your baby's cries.

There are ways to build your patience so you have more each day. Here are a few ideas:

Have compassion for the "newbies." Both you and your baby are new at this, and learning is a process that takes time and practice. You don't expect to understand all of the facets of a new job on day one, and parenting is similar in that you're needing to learn new skills to parent your child. Even if you have older children, you're still discovering new aspects about *this* child every day – learning about her temperament, frustrations, and joys. Familiarize yourself with what your child is capable of developmentally (see the list in Chapter Two) to understand what you can expect from your child at different ages. That will help build your patience, too.

To reduce stress, do less. In my coaching practice, I help moms figure out what they can ditch or delegate from their to-do lists. Letting go of what you don't want to do can free up time, energy, and inner resources so you can be more positive and patient. The best way to clear your task list of the extra weight is to rank your to-do items by both importance and desirability. Look at each chore and decide how important it is for the smooth running of your household, and how desirable is it for you personally. Tasks that are both low in importance and low in desirability are perfect for ditching. For example, how important and desirable is it that dinners are homemade? Can you ditch a lot of the prep work and warm up healthy frozen food a few nights a week instead? Responsibilities that are high in importance but low in desirability need to be done, but not necessarily by you. These tasks are great to delegate, like having the grocery shopping done by an outside company or hiring a cleaner to tackle the bathrooms.

Build brain power in other ways. You can bring your brain's executive director back into the board room – even when you haven't been sleeping well – by getting regular exercise, eating healthily, and adding a bit of mindfulness to your day. Even if you spend only a few minutes a day taking a short walk with your baby, making healthy choices about meals, or bringing your attention to your breath while doing the dishes, your brain will benefit and you'll have more resources to draw upon when you find your patience waning.

Develop awareness of your own process. When my children were younger, I found it really hard to hold onto my patience. I felt like I was doing okay throughout the day, right up until the final straw – like when my older son bit his younger brother – and I'd lose my temper and start yelling. I hated getting to that point, but didn't know what to do about it. The director at my son's nursery school gave me good advice by suggesting I create a Patience Jar by filling a glass jar with marbles to represent a stash of patience. Every time I felt frustrated, I would take a marble out of the jar. When I used my Patience Jar, I became much more aware of how the little annoyances throughout the day added up, depleting my store of patience. I realized that even if I wasn't sleeping well, I could still do things to add more marbles back into the jar, like going outside for a walk or taking mental breaks throughout the day. By making little changes in not only to how I managed my day but how I managed myself, I learned something important: the Patience Jar wasn't only for my children, it was for me, too.

"Have patience with all things," said Saint Francis de Sales. "But, first of all with yourself."

Chapter Eight
Signing in Special Circumstances

Signing Story: Sign Language is Invaluable

"Cora was born and immediately taken away to the NICU. Fortunately, she only stayed 24 hours, but soon after that we found out she did not pass the newborn hearing screening test in the hospital. When Cora was two days old, we found out that she was hard of hearing. We were swimming through the challenges of living with a newborn and, on top of that, going to seemingly endless doctor appointments to find out the extent of her hearing challenges. She now has hearing aids, which boost her hearing abilities, but there are still times she can't catch everything going on in a conversation. In noisy restaurants or across a distance, sign language has been invaluable. If she's having a hard day and takes out her hearing aids, we can still communicate, thanks to sign language."

– Robin

When Signing is Necessary and Needed

Signing with your baby can be a fun activity for your family and a useful tool to help your baby communicate her needs and desires long before she can verbally speak. But signing with your child can be much more than a fun tool; it can be a necessary and needed resource. In circumstances when a child experiences a language or developmental delay or when there's a special needs situation, sign language can ease communication barriers, provide a way for a non-verbal child to communicate, create a path for learning, and provide many other benefits for children and their families.

Research studies have proven the benefits of signing with children who have an autism spectrum disorder, Down syndrome, apraxia of speech, and other special needs issues. A paper published in the *Journal of Autism and Developmental Disorders* showed that children on the autism spectrum and children with Down syndrome understand the meaning of signs as well as conventionally developing children, even if the children with autism or Down syndrome can't replicate the signs. Another study showed that when sign language was combined with verbal speech with children with Down syndrome, their receptive language skills (what the children could comprehend) and expressive language abilities (what the children could communicate either verbally or with signs) were enhanced. Integrating sign language with assistive technology, body language, and other communicative tools is called "total communication," and is highly beneficial for children of all abilities to increase their ability to communicate.

> "Our daughter is on the autism spectrum. She needs prompting for some social interactions, such as using manners, when to listen, and when to wait for her turn. With sign language, I'm able to guide her without interrupting or being intrusive."
> – Samantha

Sometimes, like in the signing story at the beginning of this chapter, a child's special needs are diagnosed early, like with a hearing loss or a diagnosis of Down syndrome. In this kind of situation, signing can be included as part of the family's plan for supporting and communicating with their child very early on.

Other special circumstances may not be diagnosed until later, like in the case of language delays, sensory processing disorders, or autism spectrum disorder diagnoses. Or a child's challenges can come unexpectedly, like as a result of an accident. In these kinds of circumstances, there's a huge benefit to the entire family when sign language is already a natural part of the family dynamic. Since a child's speech center is wired in the early months of life, that is a fundamental time for a child to learn how words are linked to objects and concepts. As far as the brain is concerned, signs are just as powerful as verbalized words for creating those links.

Many special-needs children learn best visually, and the iconic nature of sign language can greatly benefit visual learners. Although a child with severe disabilities may not grasp the concepts imbedded in the meanings of signs as well as a mildly or moderately disabled child can, studies show that signing still has its benefits, like creating communication pathways for children who aren't as able to communicate orally.

If your child has special needs, you'll most likely receive early intervention from physicians, speech therapists, occupational therapists, and other experts about the best ways to communicate with your child. The recommendations included throughout this book about how to sign with your child may be helpful, too.

Here are some additional ideas about how to incorporate sign language when there are special circumstances in your family:

Adjust your expectations. As I've mentioned, your child will start to sign on her own timeline. You'll know your child is getting ready to sign when she starts clapping her hands or waving goodbye, because these gestures are indicative of fine motor development.

When your child signs back, he might make the signs differently than you're signing them to him. Many signs require a complicated arrangement of gross and fine motor skills and coordination, so your child may have a different "pronunciation" once he begins to sign back to you. The movements may be different and the hand shapes might not look the same, but the most important thing is that you're communicating. You can keep showing your child the correct way to sign by repeating the sign back to him, staying positive the whole time.

Start with the signs you most need your child to know. These can be cautionary signs, like *careful, wait,* and *listen.* Other good signs to include when you first start signing are words for people, food, objects, and activities that are a part of your daily routines, like *eat, milk, Mommy, Daddy, medicine,* and *more.* Other signs to include in their early vocabulary are signs for what interests your child the most, whether it's *trucks* and *trains* or *rainbows* and *kitty cats.* To encourage more complete communication, combine the signs with verbalization of the words whenever you sign. Also, try to link the words and signs with the objects, actions, or concepts by showing pictures, holding objects, pointing, and making sure you're timing the sign with the activity. This helps your child gain understanding about the meanings of the words.

Don't wait for your child to sign back before teaching additional signs. Receptive language begins before expressive language – and expressive language skills aren't an indicator of comprehension. It's often far from the truth to assume that a child can't understand language because he isn't communicating verbally or with signs.

"When my son Robert was born we found out he had Down syndrome. We started Early Intervention Services when he was six months old and the therapists there encouraged us to start signing with him. What a lifesaver! When Robert turned three and entered the public school system, a speech therapist told us to stop signing because it would delay his verbal development. Luckily, I'd already seen the power of signing. Since it was my only form of communication with my son, I was not going to give it up! Robert is now 17 years old and verbal, but when I'm not able to clearly understand him, he fingerspells or signs to tell me what he wants me to know."

– **Teri** (baby sign language instructor)

Chapter Eight Quick Tip: Home Signs

What if your child is pointing and pointing at a bright red truck on the street, but you can't remember the sign for truck? If you don't have this book on your smartphone or in your diaper bag, it's okay to create your own sign, so you can give your child a sign right then for what he's excited about. It's best to stay true to ASL as much as possible, so that you have a system for staying consistent, but it's not uncommon, even in a Deaf family, to have non-standard signs, commonly called "home signs."

When I showed my oldest son the ASL sign for *truck*, I positioned my hands like I was holding on to a big steering wheel. After I demonstrated the ASL sign, I playfully made the motion of a trucker pulling the cord to the horn, and made a big honking noise. The honking gesture and noise was what stuck. My son continued to do my silly home sign for truck instead of the ASL sign – and he included the sound effect, too.

However you sign different words with your child, try to stay consistent so as to help your child learn more easily. The most important thing to remember is that you're using signs to communicate more with your child, not to build ASL fluency – although if you continue your studies in ASL, you'll have a lot of company, as ASL is now the third most studied language in the United States.

Kathleen's Coaching Corner

What to Expect

"Expectation doesn't stop painful stuff from happening;
it just blames it on someone else."
– Heather Marshall

Motherhood may not look anything like what you dreamed it would look like before you gave birth. If there are vast differences between how you imagined your life would be and the reality of how motherhood really is, that can create a lot of unhappiness.

A study from the early 1990s looked at women's expectations of motherhood, first in the pre-baby stage and then a year after giving birth. The study's author, an Australian nurse named Carol McVeigh, discovered that the higher the expectations a woman had going into motherhood about what being a mom would be like and how much other people would help, the more disappointed that mom became in the year after giving birth, regardless of her circumstances or how much support was available to her.

Expectations throughout motherhood can negatively influence your perception of your life. Your expectations of how your day to day routines should go, how much other people should help, and even how much work and chores you should be able to get done in a day, can color how you perceive your life.

Too high expectations of yourself and others can make your life look dark, like wearing sunglasses when the sun has already gone down.

Expectations are often well-intentioned. People use expectations to try to control their perceptions of outside environments in the hopes that they'll feel more at peace within. When you expect that your mom is going to stay for three weeks to help care for your new baby, or that your husband will shelve his long-distance running hobby until after the baby is past the colicky phase, it's as if you're trying to make changes from the outside in: *If I have more help, then I'll be happier.* When you expect other people to make you happy, you're destined for disappointment. Happiness is always an inside job.

Here are three ways to get those messy expectations out of the way and free up the path to more happiness:

Clean up your language. A way to begin to see how expectations might be creating a dark film on your rose-colored glasses is by noticing when you're using "dirty" words, like *should, supposed to,* and *have to.* When these words find their way into your thoughts and conversations, they signal the presence of expectations about how life is supposed to unfold.

Dirty words also establish obligations about how people – including yourself – should behave, which often leads to disappointment when the outcome is different than what you expected. Shifting from dirty words to cleaner ones – like *want to, choose to, will,* and *can* – shifts expectations to something much lighter, like having a wish or a desire.

Here's an example: *My mother should stay for three weeks to help* shifts to *I want my mother to stay for three weeks to help.* By getting clear about what you want, you create the opportunity to ask for it, instead of letting resentment build behind your *shoulds* and *supposed-tos.*

Examine your thoughts. When you're frustrated or using the "dirty" words, take a moment to question the thought by asking yourself, "Is that true?" The answer to this simple question can change your world from the inside out. For example, when you question your thought *My husband should shelve his long-distance running training* by asking, "Is it true?" you might be able to see that you *want* him to be home to help you with the baby, which is different from *expecting* him to stop doing what he loves. "Taking responsibility for your beliefs and judgments gives you the power to change them," writes Byron Katie, creator of The Work, a process that helps people to identify and question their thoughts to create more happiness from within.

Trust that things will fall into place. Trusting yourself and trusting that circumstances will work out can be challenging, especially when you're a new (or even an experienced) mom, and particularly when everything is always changing because your child keeps growing and developing. What used to work to put your baby to sleep no longer does, because now he's teething and cranky. His once very predictable nap schedule has become completely unpredictable, because he's outgrown his morning nap. If you have a child with special needs, unpredictability can rule your schedule and your life.

When you trust that things will fall into place, you believe that everything will be okay, that the right people will show up when you need them, and that you can do hard things and grow stronger. When you trust, you stop letting worry drive the train of thoughts that often rule – and ruin – your days.

One of my favorite mottos is "Worry is prayer for what you don't want." I repeat this phrase regularly when I find myself getting worked up by my expectations of myself and other people, when I start thinking that my little plan for my life is more important than the bigger one that I can't always see, and when the destination becomes more important than the journey itself. As Ursula Le Guin wrote: "It is good to have an end to journey toward; but it is the journey that matters, in the end."

Chapter Nine

Happily Ever After

Signing Story: When You Can't Quite Understand What Your Child is Saying

"Frequently, when I can't quite understand what my daughter, River, who's 26 months old, is saying she'll repeat it over and over verbally. I'll ask if she can sign it instead, and often she can and that helps me understand her. I believe that signing and talking to River has really boosted her understanding and sped her verbal skills. As she talks these days, she frequently throws in signs as part of her normal vocabulary. She signs lots of animals, colors, foods, and cars, as well as sounds we hear but can't see, like *sirens*, *thunder*, *bird*, *dog*, *cat*, and the list goes on and on. My daughter's verbal skills came early – at about 12 months, along with her use of signs – and now, at 26 months, she is using long, complex sentences of up to ten words. Signing isn't easy for me, but whenever I sign with River, I can almost feel the new pathways being opened in my brain."

– Shawn

What the Dickens Are You Trying to Say?

As your child matures and starts to speak verbally, she'll go through a transitional period, speaking some words and signing others, and combining signs and spoken words, too. As your child becomes more and more verbal, she'll generally and naturally drop signs once she can verbalize the words. Signing is to talking like crawling is to walking. As soon your baby can walk, she'll be thrilled that she can get from one place to another so quickly. She'll experience the same thrill when her signing transitions to verbalizing.

However, when your child is two or three years old, it can be really hard to understand what your child is trying to tell you. When you encourage the use of sign language – even once your child starts talking verbally – you have another pathway for your child to communicate with you as she's coordinating all of the different mechanisms to put verbal speech together. Asking your child if she can use her hands to tell you what she wants when you can't quite understand what she's trying to say verbally can reduce her frustration and minimize the temper tantrums and make the "terrible twos" and "horrible threes" not as much of an ordeal for you or your child.

Kathleen and I continued to sign with our children even after they spoke verbally. The fact that our sons knew how to sign fostered great communication throughout toddlerhood, and signing came to our rescue many times.

I remember one of my older son's long stroller walks when he was a toddler. Even though he had been speaking verbally for several months, I couldn't always understand him. While on the walk, my son demanded, "Mush! Mush!" I sped up the pace, pushing the stroller more quickly, thinking that my son had somehow learned the dog-sledding command to make dogs run faster. But going faster wasn't what my son wanted. He kept saying, "Mush! Mush!" and I could hear in his voice that he was getting more and more frustrated. I stopped the stroller and asked him to say what he wanted more slowly. Getting even more exasperated, he replied, very slowly, "Muuuuuusssshhhh." Still confused, I asked him if he could tell me what he wanted with his hands. My son beat his chest with his fists, signing *gorilla*, and I instantly understood what he wanted: the "munch" cereal with the picture of a gorilla on the box, which we kept in the bottom of the stroller.

I put some cereal on the tray of my son's stroller and he munched (mushed) happily all the way home. Crisis averted!

Signing can save the day in so many ways: it can alleviate frustration when your toddler can't find the right words to say out loud; you can ask a personal question (about the need to use the bathroom, for example) without embarrassment; and you can encourage better behavior without drawing others' attention, by signing *wait, listen, stop, please,* or *thank you.*

Here are more ways that continuing to sign can benefit your child and your family:

Feel the phonics. Learning how to sign is beneficial for all age groups, not only for babies, because signing helps the brain to learn. Since a signing child can not only hear the words but also see and feel them, she uses more brain power to access and remember information. Teaching elementary school-aged children how to fingerspell the alphabet helps them build their vocabularies, read faster, and score higher on spelling tests. Signing can also improve dyslexic students' reading abilities, helping them to spell, isolate sounds, and sound out words.

Signing clearly demonstrates that motor memory is different from auditory recall. One parent who went through our program shared a story about her daughter, who is dyslexic and skilled at ASL, who repeatedly scored 100 percent on her spelling tests. The daughter said, "Mom, I just fingerspelled the words!" When children use ASL to study for spelling tests, fingerspelling helps them to "feel the phonics" and then, later, remember how to spell the words.

Teachers have white boards handy in the classrooms, which is super helpful for visual learners. Fingerspelling is like having your own white board with you wherever you go. Parents and children can fingerspell the letters as the child sounds out the words. Fingerspelling can help older children as they learn to read. For kinesthetic learners – those who learn by doing – fingerspelling and signing can help to channel physical energy into communicating their thoughts.

"Motor memory is a powerful thing. When I was teaching an after-school ASL class, I had a third grade student who flew through the alphabet. She stared at her hand and exclaimed, "I don't know how it knows what to do." I told her to check with her parents to see if she learned ASL when she was little. Sure enough, she had attended a preschool where they sang and signed the alphabet every morning."

– Teri (baby sign language instructor)

Signing saves you from shouting. Signing is great to use when you're in a noisy situation, like a busy playground, because it reduces the need to shout. Whether you want to communicate to your child that it will be time to go in five minutes, or to send a gentle reminder to be careful climbing the ladder to the slide, you can sign to your child from all the way across the playground.

In our family, we're all trained to pay attention when one of us whistles two distinct tones, what we call our "family whistle." When we hear that whistle, we all know it's time to "listen with our eyes," because someone is going say something with their hands. That whistle was especially helpful when the kids were younger, playing on the other side of the playground, had wandered a bit too far up the path on a hike, or were engrossed in an activity at the kids' gym but it was time to head for home.

"I still use the signs for *sit down now* or *stop* when my daughter needs to not only hear it but see it. When there is a lot of stimulation and she sees me signing, I feel like she can comprehend the meaning better."

– Julieta

Signing can give your family its own secret language. Your child, or even your partner, can silently sign when he's headed to the restroom, avoiding announcing the trip to everyone. Our sons still sign *I love you*, their discrete way to show affection to us in front of their friends. But before you start signing any thoughts you don't want to share with everyone, remember that ASL is one of the most popular languages in the nation and you might have eavesdroppers!

Chapter Nine Quick Tip: Go All In

Your child is a natural mimic. If you wave your arms around when you talk, your child is going to wave her arms around, too. If you talk with your hands on your hips, your son will, too. Mimicry is one of the earliest skills your child develops, as evidenced by studies that show infants – some only hours old – mimicking grown-ups' facial expressions.

With sign language, if you do small, wimpy signs with your baby, he'll do small, wimpy signs back. Trust me – it will be impossible to understand him with his tiny hands and limited motor skills if that happens. Avoid "mumbling" when you sign, slow down, and make your signs very distinct. When you sign *cat*, imagine the elongated whiskers on a tiger. When you sign *elephant*, make the sign and the sound as enormous as the elephant itself. When you sign *drink*, think Oktoberfest and tilt your head back like you're taking a big swallow. Not only will you make signing more fun for your child – because what child doesn't like seeing a grown-up act silly? – you'll be giving them an example of how to be playful and enjoy life to the fullest.

Kathleen's Coaching Corner

Shortcuts to Happiness

"I realized something no one tells you: that a child is a grenade.
When you have a baby, you set off an explosion in your marriage,
and when the dust settles, your marriage is different from what it
was. Not better, necessarily; not worse, necessarily; but different."
– Nora Ephron

No one really tells us this before the baby is born – or maybe we just aren't
ready to hear it: children wreak havoc on a marriage. The statistics of what
happens to a marriage once the baby comes are pretty dismal: about two-
thirds of couples see the quality of their relationship drop within three years
of the birth of a child; 92 percent of parents with children describe a gradual
increase in conflict after having a baby; almost one in four couples indicate
that their marriage is in distress by the time their baby is 18 months old – and
that doesn't include the 13 percent who have already announced separations
or divorces.

Is it inevitable that your happiness within your marriage will vanish, now
that you're challenged by the time, attention, and resources that your baby
demands? The answer to that question depends on a number of factors, like how
much effort you're willing to put into your marriage, how much time you can set
aside for your partner, and how much you want your marriage to work.

When our children were little, Bill's and my marriage fit into the dismal statistics listed above. I had waited so long to become a mother, and I wanted children so intensely, that I was determined to be *the very best mom*. I put my children first – because that's what a "good mom" does – but I didn't realize the disastrous effects that would have on my relationship with Bill. The more engrossed I became with our children, the more Bill and I bickered and fought. We found a way to argue about just about everything, but what we fought about most was who did more: who folded more clothes, who changed more diapers, who worked harder, and on and on. I wish I knew then what I know now: no one wins at that game.

I realized that my marriage needed repairing, so I did what I always do when I have a problem that needs to be solved: I started doing research. I discovered the work of John Gottman, considered to be the relationship expert in the United States. I began reading his book, *The Seven Principles for Making Marriage Work*, plus everything I could find online about what he recommended to rebuild a relationship.

In his book, Gottman recommends that a couple spend five hours a week on their relationship. He calls this the "Five Magic Hours." When I read about the Five Magic Hours and thought about my life with small children, I knew why Gottman called those hours "magic" – there had to be some sprinkling of fairy dust or a waving of wands to reveal five more hours in a week. I couldn't even find five extra minutes.

I dropped the book right then and there, overwhelmed with the thought of what I'd have to do with my schedule in order to find five more hours each week for my relationship. But our marriage was in crisis and needed help, so Bill and I found a couples counselor and started seeing her regularly for counseling sessions. That was the best thing for our marriage. Bill and I filled our marital tool belt with ideas and resources to help mend our marriage, and we came out the other side of counseling stronger and better able to withstand the stormy seas of co-parenting. Between our counseling appointments and homework, we probably ended up spending five hours a week on our marriage – and I did need to do some fancy footwork with childcare in order to make room for the sessions. Restoring our marriage, however, was worth every minute.

Back then, we would have preferred to use those Five Magic Hours on date nights, quiet conversations, and long hikes through the redwoods without children complaining, "When can we go home?" instead of sitting in a counselor's office. Even these days, Bill and I spend most of our time together working instead of connecting in other ways.

It's challenging to find *together time* when we're busy and distracted by work, our children, and all of our other commitments. What I've discovered, however, is that there are shortcuts to a happy marriage. Through couples counseling with Bill, in the process of researching and writing my first book, *The Well-Crafted Mom*, in my training to become a certified life coach, and in my life coaching work with moms, I've found three great shortcuts to a happy, healthy relationship:

Shortcut One: Give Hugs. Psychologist Virginia Satir said that people need four hugs a day for survival, eight for maintenance, and 12 to be at their best emotionally. When you hug someone for at least 20 seconds, the hormone oxytocin is released in both you and the person on the other side of the hug. Oxytocin is the same hormone that's released when you breastfeed, have skin-to-skin contact with your baby, when you're intimate with your partner, and even when you give your baby – or your spouse – a massage. Oxytocin is called the *love hormone*, because it facilitates bonding, creates feelings of closeness, and even makes people more generous. When you do the math of multiplying 12 hugs a day by 20 seconds per hug, you get a total of four minutes. That's the shortcut to increasing the connection in your marriage: spending four minutes a day – in 20 second increments – hugging.

Shortcut Two: Turn Toward. John Gottman (yes, I picked his book back up again) talks about *bids* in relationships. Bids are the small efforts that partners make to connect with each other throughout the day. These requests for attention can come in many different forms, like your partner talking about a frustrating coworker, commenting on the ball game, or sharing a story about your son. "Real-life romance is fueled by a far more humdrum approach to staying connected," writes Gottman. "It is kept alive each time you let your spouse know he or she is valued during the grind of everyday life."

When your partner makes a bid for attention, you can respond in one of three ways: you can ignore him, deny the bid by getting angry or resentful, or turn toward him. When you respond to your partner's bid for attention by turning toward him and making eye contact, answering a question, or acknowledging what he has to say, you are contributing greatly to your shared emotional bank account. This only takes a few minutes to do and is a powerful shortcut to a happy marriage.

Shortcut Three: Be Generous. Small acts of kindness, like giving foot rubs, taking the heavy basket of laundry upstairs, or making your spouse a cup of coffee, can have a positive impact on your marriage and create what W. Bradford Wilcox from the University of Virginia calls *generosity*. In this case, generosity doesn't mean giving lavish gifts. Wilcox, director of the National Marriage Project, defines generosity as "small acts of kindness, displays of respect and affection, and a willingness to forgive one's spouse his or her faults and failings." Wilcox's study found that the happiest couples are the most generous couples: 50 percent of people who ranked high in generosity reported their marriages as being very happy; only 14 percent of people who scored lower on generosity evaluations claimed to have very happy marriages. The shortcut to a very happy marriage? Do little, kind things for your partner every day.

It may seem like you need a little bit of magic to keep your marriage – or other aspects of your life – together. What I've learned, however, is that the magic isn't calculated by the hours you spend with your husband or with your child. The magic is always in the meaning you infuse into the moment that's right here in front of you: the delighted baby watching you make a hugely exaggerated sign for *dance* as you both cavort around the room, the slightly surprised spouse who notices you turning toward him and sympathetically signing *poor you* as he vents his frustrations about work, or the unexpected moment when everyone's asleep and you still have some energy left over to enjoy yourself in the peace and quiet of your home.

When you pay attention to what's *right here/right now*, that's where you'll find your shortcuts – in your marriage, in your parenthood, and in your life – one after the other on your path to happily ever after.

Endnotes

Introduction

Rachel H. Thompson, Nicole M. Cotnoir-Bichelman, Paige M. McKerchar, Trista L. Tate, and Kelly A. Dancho, "Enhancing Early Communication through Infant Sign Training." *Journal of Applied Behavior Analysis*, 40:1 (Spring, 2007): 15–23. DOI: 10.1901/jaba.2007.23-06.

Chapter One

J. Cyne Johnston, Andrée Durieux-Smith, and Kathleen Bloom, "Teaching Gestural Signs to Infants to Advance Child Development: A Review of the Evidence." *First Language*, 25:2 (2005): 235-251. DOI: 10.1177/0142723705050340.

Marilyn Daniels, "The Effects of Sign Language on Hearing Children's Language Development." *Communication Education*, 43 (October, 1994): 291-298. DOI: 10.1080/03634529409378987.

Adam Marcus, "Speech, Sign Language All the Same to Brain Communication. Modes Light Up Same Centers," *Pursuit of Research*, July 10, 2012. http://

pursuitofresearch.org/2012/07/10/sign-language-pecs-as-communication-and-a-way-to-reduce-frustration-for-speech-impaired.

Linda Acredolo and Susan Goodwyn, "Symbolic Gesturing in Normal Infants." *Child Development*, 59 (1988): 450-466. DOI: 10.2307/1130324.

Susan Goodwyn, Linda P. Acredolo, and Catherine A. Brown, "Impact of Symbolic Gesturing on Early Language Development." *Journal of Nonverbal Behavior*, 24:2 (Summer, 2000): 81-103. DOI: 10.1023/A:1006653828895.

Marilyn Daniels, "Seeing Language: The Effect Over Time of Sign Language on Vocabulary Development in Early Childhood Education." *Child Study Journal*, 26 (1996): 193-208. http://eric.ed.gov/? id=ED392103.

Claire D. Vallotton and Catherine C. Ayoub, "Symbols Build Communication and Thought: The Role of Gestures and Words in the Development of Engagement Skills and Social-Emotional Concepts During Toddlerhood." *Social Development*, 19:3 (August 2010): 601-626. DOI: 10.1111/j.1467-9507.2009.00549.x.

Thompson, Cotnoir-Bichelman, McKerchar, Tate, and Dancho.

Linda Acredolo and Susan Goodwyn, *Baby Signs: How to Talk with Your Baby Before Your Baby Can Talk* (Chicago: Contemporary Books, 2002).

Linda Acredolo and Susan Goodwyn, "The Long-Term Impact of Symbolic Gesturing During Infancy on IQ at Age Eight." *Paper presented at the meetings of the International Society for Infant Studies,* (2000): Brighton, U.K.

Jill Churchill, quoted on *The Artful Parent*, "Nine of the Best Mother Quotes." http://artfulparent.com/2014/05/the-best-mother-quotes.html.

Karen Maezen Miller, *Momma Zen: Walking the Crooked Path of Motherhood* (Boston: Shambhala Publications, Inc., 2006), 141.

Vi-An Nguyen, "Mayim Bialik on Dealing with Divorce and Hopes for Amy and Sheldon on The Big Bang Theory" *Parade*, June 6, 2013. http://parade.com/20215/viannguyen/mayim-bialik-on-dealing-with-divorce-and-hopes-for-amy-and-sheldon-on-the-big-bang-theory.

Chapter Two

Jennifer Welsh, "Six-Month-Old Infants Understand Words." *LiveScience.com*, February 14, 2012. http://www.livescience.com/18469-infants-understand-words.html.

Elika Bergelsona and Daniel Swingley, "At 6–9 Months, Human Infants Know the Meanings of Many Common Nouns." *Proceedings of the National Academy of Sciences of the United States of America*, 109:9 (February 28, 2012): 3253–3258. DOI: 10.1073/pnas.1113380109.

Carolyn Brockmeyer Cates, Benard P. Dreyer, Samantha B. Berkule, Lisa J. White, Jenny A. Arevalo, and Alan L. Mendelsohn, "Infant Communication and Subsequent Language Development in Children from Low Income Families: The Role of Early Cognitive Stimulation." *Journal of Developmental and Behavioral Pediatrics*, 33:7 (September, 2012): 577–585. DOI: 10.1097/DBP.0b013e318264c10f.

LaTasha Ortiz, "Baby Signing: How ASL Improves Language Development." LifePrint.com, December 12, 2006. http://www.lifeprint.com/asl101/topics/babysigning5.htm.

Judith Graham and Leslie A. Forstadt, "Children and Brain Development: What We Know About How Children Learn." *University of Maine, Cooperative Extension Publications, Bulletin #4356*, 2011. https://extension.umaine.edu/publications/4356e.

"Stages of Speech and Language Development." *TalkingPoint.org*, 2007. http://www.talkingpoint.org.uk/sites/talkingpoint.org.uk/files/stages-speech-language-development-chart001.pdf.

Larry Fenson, Philip S. Dale, J. Steven Reznick, Elizabeth Bates, Donna J. Thal, Stephen J. Pethick, Michael Tomasello, Carolyn B. Mervis and Joan Stiles, "Variability in Early Communicative Development." *Monographs of the Society for Research in Child Development*, 59:5 (1994): 1-185. DOI: 10.2307/1166093.

Julia Glass, "Nature vs. Nurture?" *Parenting.com*. http://www.parenting.com/article/nature-vs-nurture.

Tanya Lewis, "Twins Separated at Birth Reveal Staggering Influence of
    Genetics." *LiveScience.com,* August 11, 2014. http://www.livescience.
    com/47288-twin-study-importance-of-genetics.html.
Thomas J. Bouchard Jr, David T. Lykken, Matt McGue, Nancy L. Segal,
    and Auke Tellegen, "Sources of Human Psychological Differences: The
    Minnesota Study of Twins Reared Apart." *Science,* 250:4978 (October 12,
    1990): 223-228. DOI: 10.1126/science.2218526.
Catherynne M. Valente, *The Girl Who Circumnavigated Fairyland in a Ship of
    Her Own Making* (New York: Macmillan, 2011), 104.
Jan Kristal, *The Temperament Perspective: Working with Children's Behavioral
    Styles* (New York: Paul H. Brookes Publishing Company, Inc., 2005).
Barbara Keogh, "How Temperament Affects Parents, Children, and
    Family Life." *GreatKids.com.* http://www.greatschools.org/gk/articles/
    temperament-affects-parents-children-family.
Harvey Karp, *The Happiest Toddler on the Block* (New York: Bantam Dell,
    2004), 33.
Susan Cain, *Quiet: The Power of Introverts in a World That Can't Stop Talking*
    (New York: Crown Publishing Group, 2012).
Jennifer Granneman, "For Extroverts: 15 Ways to Be a Better Parent to Your
    Introverted Kid." *QuietRevolution.com.* http://www.quietrev.com/15-ways-
    to-parent.

Chapter Three

Michael Morales, Peter Mundy, Christine E.F. Delgado, Marygrace Yale, Daniel
    Messinger, Rebecca Neal, and Heidi Schwartz, "Responding to Joint
    Attention Across the 6- through 24-Month Age Period and Early Language
    Acquisition." *Journal of Applied Developmental Psychology,* 21 (2000):
    283–298. DOI:10.1016/S0193-3973(99)00040-4.
Tricia Striano, Xin Chen, Allison Cleveland, and Stephanie Bradshaw,
    "Joint Attention Social Cues Influence Infant Learning." *European
    Journal of Developmental Psychology,* 3:3 (2006): 289–299. DOI:
    10.1080/17405620600879779.

Brie Moore, Linda Acredolo, and Susan Goodwyn, "Symbolic Gesturing and Joint Attention: Partners in Facilitating Verbal Development." *Paper presented at the Biennial Meetings of the Society for Research in Child Development,* April 2001.

Michael Tomasello, Malinda Carpenter, and Ulf Liszkowski, "A New Look at Infant Pointing." *Child Development,* 78:3 (May/June, 2007): 705-772. Stable URL: http://www.jstor.org/stable/4620661.

Ulf Liszkowski, Malinda Carpenter, and Michael Tomasello, "Reference and Attitude in Infant Pointing." *Journal of Child Language,* 34 (2007): 1-20. DOI:10.1017/S0305000906007689.

Ulf Liszkowski, Malinda Carpenter, Anne Henning, Tricia Striano, and Michael Tomasello, "Twelve-Month-Olds Point to Shared Attention and Interest." *Developmental Science,* 7:3 (2004):297-307. http://www.ncbi. nlm.nih.gov/pubmed/15595371.

Nairán Ramírez-Esparza, Adrián García-Sierra, and Patricia K. Kuhl, "Look Who's Talking: Speech Style and Social Context in Language Input to Infants are Linked to Concurrent and Future Speech Development." *Developmental Science,* 17:6 (November, 2014): 880–891. DOI: 10.1111/ desc.12172.

Anne Fernald, "Four-Month-Old Infants Prefer to Listen to Motherese." *Infant Behavior and Development,* 8:2 (April-June, 1985): 181-195. DOI:10.1016/S0163-6383(85)80005-9.

Oscar Wilde, quoted on *Goodreads,* "Oscar Wilde > Quotes > Quotable Quote," https://www.goodreads.com/quotes/336524-the-best-way-to-make-children-good-is-to-make.

University of Washington, "Babies' Brains Show that Social Skills Linked to Second Language Learning." *ScienceDaily,* July 27, 2015. http://www. sciencedaily.com/releases/2015/07/150727100024.htm.

Darcia Narvaeza, Lijuan Wanga, and Ying Chenga, "The Evolved Developmental Niche in Childhood: Relation to Adult Psychopathology and Morality." *Applied Developmental Science,* (Published online January 16, 2016). DOI: 10.1080/10888691.2015.1128835.

Jenifer Goodwin, "Nurturing Moms May Help Their Child's Brain Develop." *HealthDay News*, January 30, 2012. http://health.usnews.com/health-news/family-health/brain-and-behavior/articles/2012/01/30/nurturing-moms-may-help-their-childs-brain-develop.

New York University Langone Medical Center, "Mother's Soothing Presence Makes Pain Go Away – And Changes Gene Activity In Infant Brain." November 18, 2014. http://nyulangone.org/press-releases/mothers-soothing-presence-makes-pain-go-away-and-changes-gene-activity-in-infant-brain.

Emma C. Sarro, Donald A. Wilson, and Regina M. Sullivan, "Maternal Regulation of Infant Brain State." *Current Biology*, 24:14 (July 2014): 1664–1669. DOI: http://dx.doi.org/10.1016/j.cub.2014.06.017.

Silvia M. Bell and Mary D. Salter Ainsworth, "Infant Crying and Maternal Responsiveness." *Child Development*, 43:4 (December, 1972): 1171-1190. DOI: 10.2307/1127506.

Bell and Ainsworth, 1184.

Thomas Bray, quoted in *World of Quotes*, "Thomas Bray Once Said…" http://www.worldofquotes.com/quote/53298/index.html.

Chapter Four

Betty Hart and Todd R. Risley, *Meaningful Differences in the Everyday Experiences of Young American Children* (Baltimore, MD: Paul Brookes Publishing Company, 1995).

Todd Risley, "Meaningful Differences in the Everyday Experiences of Young American Children."

Kimberly Kopko, "Research Sheds Light on How Babies Learn and Develop Language." *Cornell University Human Development Outreach & Extension*, PDF. http://www.human.cornell.edu/hd/outreach-extension/upload/casasola.pdf.

Beverly Otto, *Literacy Development in Early Childhood: Reflective Teaching for Birth to Age Eight* (Long Grove, IL: Waveland Press, 2015), 9.

Fenson, Dale, Reznick, Bates, Thal, Pethick, Tomasello, Mervis, and Stiles.

Leo J. Burke, quoted on *Quote Garden*, "Quotations about Sleep." http://www.quotegarden.com/sleep.html.

Harvey Karp, *The Happiest Baby Guide to Great Sleep* (New York: HarperCollins Publishers, 2012), 142, 161.

Jodi A. Mindell, Lorena S. Telofski, Benjamin Wiegand, and Ellen S. Kurtz, "A Nightly Bedtime Routine: Impact on Sleep in Young Children and Maternal Mood." *Sleep*, 32:5 (May 1, 2009): 599–606.

Karp, 72-73.

Ruth Feldman, Zehava Rosenthal, and Arthur I. Eidelman, "Maternal-Preterm Skin-to-Skin Contact Enhances Child Physiologic Organization and Cognitive Control Across the First 10 Years of Life." *Biological Psychiatry*, 75:1 (January 1, 2014): 56–64.

Chapter Five

Linda Groves Gillespie, "Why Do Babies Like Boxes Best?" *National Association for the Education of Young Children: Beyond the Journal / Young Children on the Web,* May, 2009. PDF. http://www.naeyc.org/files/yc/file/200905/BTJRockRoll.pdf.

Amelia Hill, "Singing to Children May Help Development of Language Skills" *The Guardian*, May 8, 2011. http://www.theguardian.com/lifeandstyle/2011/may/08/singing-children-development-language-skills.

Sally Goddard Blythe, *The Genius of Natural Childhood: Secrets of Thriving Children.* (Stroud, UK: Hawthorn Press, July 1, 2011).

Aimee E. Stahl and Lisa Feigenson, "Observing the Unexpected Enhances Infants' Learning and Exploration. *Science*, 348:6230 (April 3, 2015): 91-94. DOI: 10.1126/science.aaa3799.

Jane Goodall, quoted on *Goodreads*, "Jane Goodall > Quotes." https://www.goodreads.com/author/quotes/18163.Jane_Goodall.

Claire Lerner and Sharon Greenip, "The Power of Play: Learning to Play from Birth to Three." *Zero to Three*, 2004. http://main.zerotothree.org/site/DocServer/ThePowerofPlay.pdf; jsessionid=73C2DA784F479ABF0A88B6037E4679A2.app234c?docID=161.

Leon Neyfakh, "What Playfulness Can Do for You: Research Discovers the Many Benefits of Being a Goofball," *The Boston Globe*, July 20, 2014. http://www.bostonglobe.com/ideas/2014/07/19/what-playfulness-can-for-you/Cxd7Et4igTLkwpkUXSr3cO/story.html.

Mihaly Csikszentmihalyi, *Flow: The Psychology of Optimal Experience*, Global Learning Communities, 2000. PDF.

Stuart Brown, *Play: How It Shapes the Brain, Opens the Imagination, and Invigorates the Soul* (New York: Penguin Group, 2009), 212.

Chapter Six

Hart and Risley.

Laura Ann Petitto, Marina Katerelos, Bronna G. Levy, Kristine Gauna, Karine Tetreault, and Vittoria Ferraro, "Bilingual Signed and Spoken Language Acquisition from Birth: Implications for the Mechanisms Underlying Early Bilingual Language Acquisition." *Journal of Child Language*, 28:2 (July, 2001): 453-496. DOI: 10.1017/S0305000901004718.

Sloan Wilson, quoted on ThinkExist.com, "Sloan Wilson Quotes." http://thinkexist.com/quotation/the_hardest_part_of_raising_a_child_is_teaching/332041.html.

Chapter Seven

Susan Goodwyn, Linda Acredolo, and Catherine Brown, "Impact of Symbolic Gesturing on Early Language Development." *Journal of Nonverbal Behavior*, 24:2 (Summer, 2000): 81-103. DOI: 10.1023/A:1006653828895.

Donna J. Thal and Stacy Tobias, "Communicative Gestures in Children With Delayed Onset of Oral Expressive Vocabulary." *Journal of Speech, Language, and Hearing Research*, 35 (December, 1992): 1281-1289. DOI:10.1044/jshr.3506.1289.

Ximena Gongora and Chamarrita Farkas, "Infant Sign Language Program Effects on Synchronic Mother-Infant Interactions." *Infant Behavior & Development*, 32:2 (April, 2009): 216-225. DOI: 10.1016/j.infbeh.2008.12.011.

Nancy Eisenberg, Qing Zhou, Tracy L. Spinrad, Carlos Valiente, Richard A. Fabes, and Jeffrey Liew, "Relations Among Positive Parenting, Children's Effortful Control, and Externalizing Problems: A Three-Wave Longitudinal Study." *Child Development*, 76:5 (September/October, 2005): 1055–1071. DOI: 10.1111/j.1467-8624.2005.00897.x.

Gwen Dewar, "The Effects of Praise: What Scientific Studies Reveal About the Right Way to Praise Kids." *Parenting Science* (2008). http://www.parentingscience.com/effects-of-praise.html - sthash.kPrWD3TB.dpuf.

Claudia M. Mueller and Carol S. Dweck, "Praise for Intelligence Can Undermine Children's Motivation and Performance." *Journal of Personality and Social Psychology*, 75:1 (July, 1998): 33-52.

Elizabeth A. Gunderson, Sarah J. Gripshover, Carissa Romero, Carol S. Dweck, Susan Goldin-Meadow, and Susan C. Levine, "Parent Praise to 1-3 Year-Olds Predicts Children's Motivational Frameworks 5 Years Later." *Child Development*, 84:5 (September, 2013): 1526–1541. DOI: 10.1111/cdev.12064

Sue A. Kelley, Celia A. Brownell, and Susan B. Campbell, "Mastery Motivation and Self-Evaluative Affect in Toddlers: Longitudinal Relations with Maternal Behavior." *Child Development*, 71:4 (July/August, 2000): 1061-71. DOI: 10.1111/1467-8624.00209.

Franklin P. Adams, quoted on *Goodreads*, "Franklin P. Adams > Quotes." https://www.goodreads.com/author/quotes/8369.Franklin_P_Adams.

Saint Francis de Sales, quoted on *Goodreads*, "Francis de Sales > Quotes." https://www.goodreads.com/author/quotes/7041089.Francis_de_Sales.

Chapter Eight

Anthony Attwood, Uta Frith, and Beata Hermelin, "The Understanding and Use of Interpersonal Gestures by Autistic and Down Syndrome Children." *Journal of Autism and Developmental Disorders*, 18:2 (June, 1988): 241-257. http://www.ncbi.nlm.nih.gov/pubmed/2970453.

Ricardo D. Barrera and Beth Sulzer-Azaroff, "An Alternating Treatment Comparison of Oral and Total Communication Training Programs with

Echolalic Autistic Children." *Journal of Applied Behavior Analysis*, 16:4 (Winter, 1983): 379-394. DOI: 10.1901/jaba.1983.16-379.

Howard Goldstein, "Communication Intervention for Children with Autism: A Review of Treatment Efficacy." *Journal of Autism and Developmental Disorders*, 32:5 (October, 2002): 373-396.

Courtney A. Wright, Ann P. Kaiser, Dawn I. Reikowsky, Megan Y. Roberts, and Janna Oetting, "Effects of a Naturalistic Sign Intervention on Expressive Language of Toddlers with Down Syndrome." *Journal of Speech, Language & Hearing Research*, 56:3 (June, 2013): 994-1008.

Ricardo D. Barrera and Beth Sulzer-Azaroff, "An Alternating Treatment Comparison of Oral and Total Communications Training Programs with Echolalic Autistic Children." *Journal of Applied Behavioral Analysis*, 16:4 (Winter, 1983): 379–394. DOI: 10.1901/jaba.1983.16-379.

Vannessa T. Mueller, "Total Communication (TC) Approach" in *Encyclopedia of Autism Spectrum Disorders*, ed. Fred R. Volkmar (New York: Springer Science+Business Media, 2013), 3138-3143. DOI: 10.1007/978-1-4419-1698-3_1708.

Kim Taylor-Deliva, "Sign Language for Your Special Needs Child." *Special-ism.com*. http://special-ism.com/sign-language-for-your-special-needs-child/#MrfbQHck3oIzg5Ce.99.

Elizabeth Weise, "Sign Language No. 4 Most Studied Foreign Language." USAToday.com, December 8, 2010. http://usatoday30.usatoday.com/news/education/2010-12-08-1Alanguages08_ST_N.htm.

David Goldberg, Dennis Looney, and Natalia Lusin, "Enrollments in Languages Other Than English in United States Institutions of Higher Education." Modern Language Association Web Publication, Fall, 2013.

Heather Marshall, "Letting Go of Expectations," *TEDxGreenville*, June 18, 2014. http://tedxtalks.ted.com/video/Letting-Go-of-Expectations-Heat.

Carol McVeigh, "Motherhood Experiences from the Perspective of First-Time Mothers," *Clinical Nursing Research*, 6:4 (November 1997): 335-348.

Ursula K. Le Guin, *The Left Hand of Darkness* (New York: Ace Books, 1979).

Chapter Nine

Marilyn Daniels, "The Effect of Sign Language on Hearing Children's Language Development." *Communication Education*, 43:4 (1994): 291-298. DOI: 10.1080/03634529409378987.

Marilyn Daniels, "Seeing Language: The Effect Over Time of Sign Language on Vocabulary Development in Early Childhood Education. *Child Study Journal*, 26:3 (September, 1996): 193-208.

Jan C. McKnight, "Using the Manual Alphabet in Teaching Reading to Learning Disabled Children." *Journal of Learning Disabilities*, 12:9 (November, 1979): 581-584. DOI: 10.1177/002221947901200904.

McCay Vernon, Joan Develin Coley, and Jan Hafer DuBois, "Using Sign Language to Remediate Severe Reading Problems." *Journal of Learning Disabilities*, 13:4 (April, 1980): 215-218. DOI: 10.1177/002221948001300408.

Andrew N. Meltzoff, "Born to Learn: What Infants Learn from Watching Us." Excerpted from Nathan A Fox and John G. Worhol (Editors), *The Role of Early Experience in Infant Development*, Johnson & Johnson Pediatric Round Table Series, 1999.

Nora Ephron, *Heartburn* (New York: Vintage Books, First Vintage Contemporaries Edition, 1996), 158.

Alyson F. Shapiro and John M. Gottman, "Effects on Marriage of a Psycho-Communicative-Educational Intervention With Couples Undergoing the Transition to Parenthood, Evaluation at 1-Year Post Intervention." *Journal of Family Communication*, 5:1 (November 13, 2009), 1-24. DOI.10.1207/s15327698jfc0501_1.

Pamela Kruger, "Staying Lovers While Raising Kids." *Parents.com,* 2003. http://www.parents.com/parenting/relationships/staying-close/staying-lovers-while-raising-kids1.

Carolyn P. Cowan and Philip A. Cowan, *When Partners Become Parents: The Big Life Change for Couples* (Mahwah, NJ: Lawrence Erlbaum Associates, 2000).

John Gottman and Nan Silver, *The Seven Principles for Making Marriage Work* (New York: Three Rivers Press, 1999), 260-261.

Carolyn Rosenblatt, "Magic Touch: Six Things You Can Do to Connect in a Disconnected World." *Forbes.com,* January 18, 2011. http://www.forbes.com/sites/carolynrosenblatt/2011/01/18/magic-touch-six-things-you-can-do-to-connect-in-a-disconnected-world/#1581a8ff65ba.

Maureen Salamon, "11 Interesting Effects of Oxytocin." *LiveScience.com,* December 3, 2010. http://www.livescience.com/35219-11-effects-of-oxytocin.html.

Zach Brittle, "T is for Turning." *The Gottman Institute,* September 30, 2014. https://www.gottman.com/blog/t-is-for-turning.

Gottman and Silver, 80.

Jeffrey Dew and W. Bradford Wilcox, "Generosity and the Maintenance of Marital Quality." *Journal of Marriage and Family,* 75 (October, 2013): 1218–1228 DOI:10.1111/jomf.12066.

Sign Language Resources

Monta Briant, *Baby Sign Language Basics* (New York: Hay House, Inc., 2009).

Joseph Garcia, *Sign With Your Baby: How to Communicate with Infants Before They Can Speak* (Seattle, WA: Northlight Communications, Inc., 2005).

Mickey Flodin, *Signing Illustrated: The Complete Learning Guide* (New York: The Berkeley Publishing Group, 2004).

Lottie Riekehof, *The Joy of Signing* (Springfield, MO: Gospel Publishing House, 1987).

Lottie Riekehof, *Talk to the Deaf* (Springfield, MO: Gospel Publishing House, 1982).

Richard A. Tennant and Mariane Gluszak Brown, *The American Sign Language Handshape Dictionary* (Washington D.C.: Gallaudet University Press, 1998).

William Vicars, EdD, ASLUniversity.com.

Penny Warner, *Signing Fun: American Sign Language Vocabulary, Phrases, Games, and Activities* (Washington D.C.: Gallaudet University Press, 2006).

Baby Signing Dictionary

Here are all the signs included in the book, as well as the ASL alphabet, numbers, and handshapes. To see the signs in action, go to happybabysignsclass.com to take the introductory baby sign language class, free to readers of this book.

ASL Alphabet

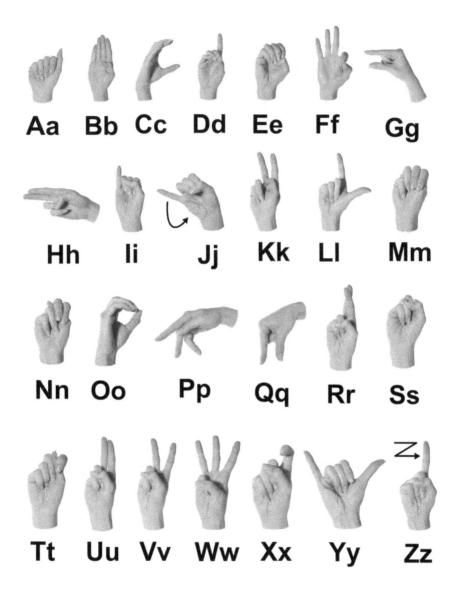

ASL Numbers

ASL Handshapes

Bent V Hand

Claw Hand

Flat O Hand

Inverted V Hand

Modified 8 Hand

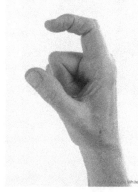

Modified C Hand

Open A Hand

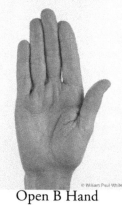

Open B Hand

ASL Signs

Airplane – [Shows shape and movement of an airplane] With a double movement, pulse the *I love you hand* (thumb, index finger, and little finger extended) over your head while making an airplane noise and saying, "Airplane."

All Done/Finished – [Symbolizes brushing something away] Beginning with both *5 hands* in front of your chest, palms facing in, flip the hands, ending with both palms facing out.

Apple – [Shows action of chewing an apple in the "apple of your cheek"] With the knuckle of the *X hand* on the cheek, twist the wrist downward with a double movement.

Baby – [Symbolizes rocking a baby in your arms] Gently swing your cradled arms, with palms facing up.

Ball – [Represents the shape of a ball] Tap the fingertips of both *claw hands* together twice in front of your chest, palms facing each other.

Balloon – [Represents blowing up a balloon] Bring the fingertips of both *claw hands* together in front of your mouth and move your hands away from each other as you make a blowing sound.

Bath – [Shows the motion of scrubbing yourself] Move the palm sides of your *A hands* up and down your chest.

Bear – [Represents a bear scratching itself] Cross your arms on your chest while scratching your shoulders and, with a grumpy face, say, "Bear. The bear says, 'Grrrr!'"

Berry – [Indicates twisting a tiny berry off the vine] Twist the tip of your non-dominant pinky between the fingers and thumb of your dominant *flat O hand*.

Bird – [Represents a bird's beak] Open and close the index finger and thumb of the *G hand* near your mouth while saying, "Bird. The bird says, 'Tweet, tweet.'"

Black – [Refers to the dark color of the eyebrows] Sweep the tip of your index finger across your forehead from the non-dominant side to the dominant side.

Blue – [Initialized sign] Twist the *B hand* at the wrist with a shaking motion.

Boat – [Shows the shape of a boat's hull going over the waves] Cup your *open B hands* together, palms facing up, and move the hands forward in a bouncing double arc.

Book – [Pretend that you are opening a book] Beginning with the palms of both *open B hands* together, open your hands by moving your thumbs apart.

Box – [Shows the four sides of a box] Hold both *open B hands* with palms facing each other, fingers pointing forward, separated by a space indicating the width of the box. Then swing both palms so they're facing your chest, with the dominant *open B hand* closest to you, to indicate the depth of the box.

Careful – [Represents eyes looking left and right] Put the dominant *K hand* on top of the non-dominant *K hand,* palms facing in opposite directions. Then, circle both hands forward, down, and back a couple times with a concerned expression on your face.

Cat – [Showing a cat's whiskers] Move both *F hands* outward from your cheeks with a double movement. Say, "Cat. The cat says 'Meow.'" If you have something in your hand, it's okay to do normally two-handed animal signs using only your free hand. This recommendation goes for most two-handed signs.

Cereal – [Represents wiping cereal off your chin] Repeatedly open and close the index finger of the *X hand* as you move your hand sideways across your chin.

Change – [Hands change positions] With the palm sides of both *X hands* together, dominant hand above non-dominant, twist the wrists in opposite directions so that the non-dominant hand is now on top of the dominant.

Cheese – [Represents grating cheese] Twist the heel of the dominant *open B hand* back and forth on the heel of the upturned non-dominant *open B hand.*

Cold – [The natural gesture of shivering] Hunch your shoulders while shaking both *S hands*, and say, "Cold," with a quivering voice.

Colors – [Fingers represent the colorful stripes of the rainbow] Wiggle the *5 hand* fingers in front of your chin.

Cry – [Shows tears flowing down your cheeks] With a sad expression, drag your index fingers alternately down your cheeks.

Daddy/Father – [Formed at the male area of the head: the forehead] With the palm facing your non-dominant side, tap the thumb of the *5 hand*, twice against your forehead.

Dance – [The little legs of a person dancing on your palm] Swing the fingers of the dominant *inverted V hand*, palm facing in, from side-to-side a couple of times over the upturned non-dominant *open B hand*.

Diaper – [Represents closing the safety pins on a diaper] With both hands at your hips, tap your index and middle fingers to your thumbs a couple times.

Dog – [A common gesture for calling a dog] Slap your dominant *open B hand* on your thigh twice and then snap the fingers of the same hand while saying, "Dog. The dog says, 'Woof, woof.'"

Down – Point index finger down with a slight movement. If you do it twice, it's the sign for *downstairs.*

Duck – [Represents a duck's bill] With the palm of your dominant hand facing forward in front of the mouth, open and close both the extended index and middle fingers onto the thumb while saying, "Duck. The duck says, 'Quack, quack.'" Another, non-ASL version of this sign is to use all four fingers to snap up and down, instead of only two fingers.

Eat/Food – [Indicates putting food in one's mouth] Bring the fingertips of the *flat O hand* toward the mouth in a movement that's repeated twice.

Elephant – [Shows the shape of an elephant's trunk] Beginning with the back of the bent *B hand* against the nose, palm facing down, move the hand down and forward with a large swooping movement while saying, "Elephant. The elephant says...." If you can, purse your lips tightly and blow to make a vibrating, high-pitched sound, as if you're making the trumpeting sound of an elephant. Babies have fun making this noise.

Fish – [Simulates the movement of a fish] With the thumb up, wiggle the *open B hand* forward while saying, "Fish. The fish says...." Pucker and make a *kissing* noise.

Frog – [Simulates a frog's legs jumping and the frog's tongue snatching a fly] Flick the fingers of the *V hand* outward to your non-dominant side with a double movement, saying, "Frog. The frog says, 'Ribbit, ribbit.'"

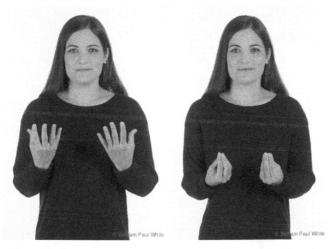

Gentle – [Indicates gentle softness] Gently move both *5 hands*, palms up, downward as you close them into *flat O hands*. Show a peaceful expression on your face as you very sweetly say, "Gentle." This is also the sign for *soft*.

Good / Night / Good Night – [*Good night* is a combination of the sign for *good* (the hand moving away from mouth) and the sign for *night* (the sun going over the horizon)] Start with the dominant *open B hand* facing your mouth. Then curve it into a bent *open B hand* as you place it palm down onto the back of your other *open B hand*.

Gorilla – [Represents a gorilla beating its chest] Alternately pound both *S hands* against the chest while saying, "Gorilla. The gorilla says 'Ooo, Ooo!'" Use a low voice for the "Ooo, Ooo!"

Grandma – [Uses the sign for *mommy*, with an added generation signified by the bouncing hand] Place the thumb of the right 5 *hand* against the chin, palm facing your non-dominant side, and bounce your hand forward, making two arcs.

Grandpa – [Uses the sign for *daddy*, with an added generation signified by the bouncing hand] Place the thumb of the right 5 *hand* against your forehead, palm facing your non-dominant side, and bounce your hand forward, making two arcs.

Green – [Initialized sign] Twist the wrist of the *G hand*.

Happy – [Represents joy rising up] Brush the palm of the *open B hand* up your chest twice while making a happy expression.

Hat – [Shows the location of a hat] Pat the top of your head twice with the *open B hand*.

Help – Place the dominant *open A hand*, thumb facing up, on top of the upturned palm of the non-dominant *open B hand*. Raise both hands up a little, as if one hand is giving the other a helping boost.

Hot – [Represents tossing away something hot from out of your mouth] With a quick motion, swing the *claw hand* from your mouth outwards while making a blowing sound.

Hungry – [Indicates the path food travels to your stomach] Drag the fingers and thumb of the *C hand* from below your throat down your chest a few inches. Remember to only make the movement once! If you repeat the motion with short quick strokes, you're signing *passion*, a more grown-up kind of hunger.

Hurt/Pain – [Represents the throbbing of pain] Pulse the index fingers toward each other several times while showing a pained expression on your face. You may twist your fingers to exaggerate the feeling. You can make the motion near the injured part of the body to show where it hurts.

I – [Establishes identify] Point to your chest.

I Love You – The abbreviated version of this sign combined the three initials *I*, *L*, and *Y* into one gesture with the *Y hand* held in front and the index finger extended up. *I love you* may also be signed as three separate signs, done in this order: *I* by pointing to the self, *love* by signing the *love* sign (see *Love*), and *you* by pointing to the other person. Don't forget to include an expression of love in your eyes!

Juice – [Initialized sign near your mouth] Place the *J hand* pinky finger near your chin and twist it toward yourself.

Jump/Hop – [Represents legs jumping] Jump the fingers of your dominant *inverted V hand* on the palm of your non-dominant *open B hand.*

Light – [The hand shows the rays of light beaming from a lamp] Elevate the *flat O hand* above your head and then open the fingers into a *5 hand.* This is an alternate version of the proper ASL sign for light.

Listen – [Common gesture of listening] Cup the ear with the bent *open B hand* facing forward.

Look – [Indicates looking at something] Hold the *V hand*, palm toward your face, then swing it around so your fingers are pointing in the direction you want your baby to look.

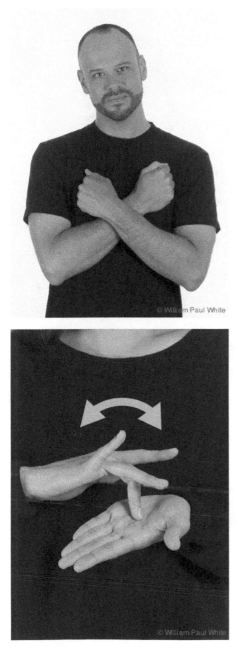

Love – [Represents giving a loving hug] Cross your fists at the wrists in front of your chest.

Medicine – [Simulates crushing herbs with a mortar and pestle] Rock the middle finger of the dominant *modified 8 hand* back and forth on the upturned non-dominant *open B hand*.

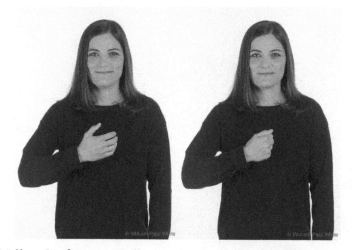

Milk – [Refers to a milking action] Open and close your fist several times.

Mine – [A common gesture for expressing possession] Place the palm of your hand on your upper chest.

Mommy/Mother – [Formed in the female area of the head: the chin] Tap the thumb of the *5 hand*, palm facing your non-dominant side, twice against your chin.

Monkey – [Shows the ribs-scratching motion monkeys do] Use the fingertips of both *claw hands* to scratch your ribs while saying, "Monkey. The monkey says, 'Eee, eee!'"

More – [Simulates gathering things together] Tap the fingertips of the *flat O hand* together twice.

Night – [Represents the sun going over the horizon] The wrist of the dominant bent *open B hand* hits twice on the back of the non-dominant *open B hand*.

No – [Combines the *N hand* and *O hand* into one abbreviated gesture] The index and middle fingers snap down on the thumb as your head shakes back and forth.

Now – Sharply drop both *Y hands* in front of you with your palms facing up. You can also use bent *open B hands*.

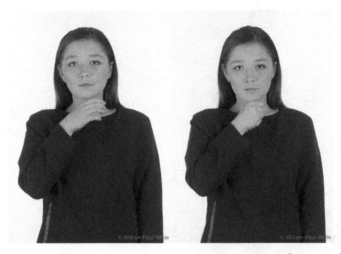

Orange – [Represents squeezing an orange near the mouth] Open and close the *S hand* in front of the chin.

Pacifier – Move the *X hand* toward your lips while making a sucking sound with your lips pursed.

Pizza – [Shows the two *Z*s in the word "pizza" with one motion] Trace a *Z* using the *bent V hand*.

Play – [The movement is loose and playful] Rotate both *Y hands* by twisting the wrists in front of your body with a repeated movement.

Please – [Symbolizes making a request from the heart] Make a counterclockwise circle with the *open B hand* over your heart.

Poop – [Represents pooping] Loosely grab the thumb of the dominant *5 hand* and move the dominant hand downward. An alternate version is to use the dominant *open A hand* instead.

Poor Baby / Sympathy – [Expresses sympathy to someone] Pulse both *modified 8 hands* forward and downward twice while making a concerned and sympathetic facial expression.

Quiet – [A common gesture of hushing for silence] Place the index finger in front of the mouth and make the "Shh" sound and then spread the *open B hands* with a downward movement.

Rainbow – [Represents the shape and stripes of a rainbow] Arc your open *5 hand* over your head.

Read – [Represents the movement of the eyes down a page] Move the fingertips of the dominant *V hand* down the palm of the non-dominant *open B hand.*

Red – [The finger indicates the redness of lips] The index finger points to the lips and then moves downward.

Run – [Represents the motion of running forward] With both *L hands*, thumbs facing up, hook the index finger of the dominant *L hand* around the thumb of the non-dominant *L hand*. Now, move the linked hands forward as you wiggle your thumbs and index fingers.

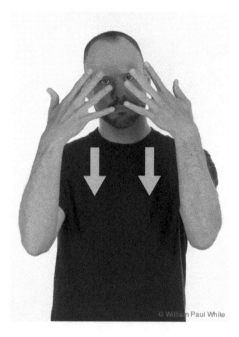

Sad – [Your hands seem to pull the face down into a sad expression] Move both *5 hands* down the sides of your face while making a sad expression.

Scared – [A common reaction of hands trying to protect the body] Both fists begin closed and then pop open toward the center of the body into open *5 hands*. Move your body back in fear as you make a frightened face.

Seal – [Shows flippers slapping together] Cross *B hands* at the wrists, both palms facing away from each other, and then slap the back of the hands together a few times and say, "Seal. The seal says, 'Argh, argh, argh.'"

See – [Indicates two eyes seeing] Place the right *V hand*, palm facing in and with the right middle finger just under the right eye, and then move the hand slightly forward.

Shoes – [Represents shoes bumping together sideways] The thumb sides of the *S hands* tap together twice.

Sing / Song / Music – [Simulates a conductor holding sheet music and conducting] Swing the dominant *open B hand* back and forth over the non-dominant *open B hand*.

Siren – [Represents flashing light on an emergency vehicle] Move the *flat O hand* in a circle repeatedly while opening and closing the fingers into a *5 hand*. This sign also means *ambulance*.

Sit – [Represents legs dangling over the edge of a chair] Set the fingers of the dominant *V hand* onto the fingers of the non-dominant *H hand*.

Sleep – [Shows a hand enticing your eyes to close] With a sleepy facial expression, bring the palm of the *5 hand* down your face to chin level, ending with a *flat O hand*.

Stop – [Indicates something coming to an abrupt halt] The little-finger edge of the dominant *open B hand* chops down on the upturned palm of the non-dominant *open B hand*.

Strawberry – [Represents the stem of a strawberry being pulled from your mouth] Place the thumb and index finger of your *F hand* at your mouth then quickly swing your hand forward while making a kissing sound.

Thank you – Move the fingertips of your dominant *open B hand* from in front of your mouth forward until your palm is facing up. It's common to smile and nod the head while making this sign.

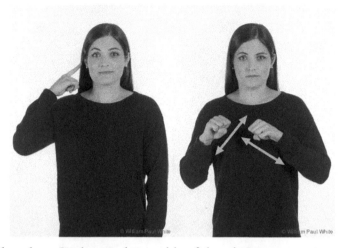

Thunder – [Indicates the rumble of thunder] Point to your ear then forcefully move both *S hands* in front of your chest with a serious face while saying in a low voice, "Boom!"

Tiger – [Represents the tiger's stripes] Place *claw hands* in front of your face, palms facing in, then draw your hands apart while saying, "Tiger. The tiger says, "Grrrr.""

Toilet / Potty – [Initialized sign] Elevate and shake your *T hand*.

Touch – [The gesture of touching something] Touch the middle finger of your dominant *modified 8 hand* to the back of your downturned non-dominant *open B hand*.

Train – [Represents the rails and cross ties on a railroad track] Rub the fingers of your dominant *H hand* back and forth on the backs of the fingers of your non-dominant *H hand* while making the "chugga chugga" sound of a train coming down the track.

Tree – [Represents the branches of a tree blowing in the wind] Place the elbow of your dominant *5 hand* on the back of your non-dominant *open B hand*. Twist the dominant *5 hand* a few times.

Truck – [Simulates holding onto a big steering wheel] Arc both *S hands* from side to side in front of your lower ribs.

Unicorn – [Represents a spiraled unicorn horn] Place the *R hand* on your forehead and move it straight up.

Up – Point your index finger up with a slight movement. If you do it twice, it means *upstairs*.

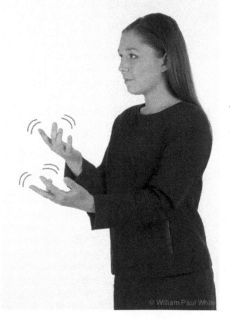

Wait – [Indicates impatience] With your dominant hand closer to you and both palms up, wiggle your fingers.

Walk – [Represents walking feet] Alternately walk both *open B hands*, palms down, in a forward motion.

Want – [Represents bringing a wanted thing toward oneself] Beginning with both *5 hands* in front of the body, palms facing up, bring the hands back toward the chest while constricting the fingers into *claw hands*.

Water – [Initialized sign near the mouth] Tap the index finger side of the *W hand*, palm facing your non-dominant side, against your chin with a double movement.

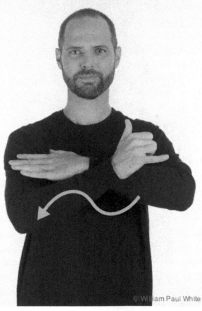

Whale – [The movement of the dominant hand represents a whale's tail and the non-dominant arm shows the surface of the ocean] Place the non-dominant forearm horizontally, palm side down, in front of your chest. Swoop your dominant *Y hand* up and down in front of your forearm, in the direction of your dominant side.

Where – [Indicates your index finger searching for something] Wag your extended index finger from side to side with your palm facing forward.

Yellow – [Initialized sign] Twist the *Y hand* at the wrist.

Yes – [Represents nodding your head] Rock your *S hand* up and down as your head nods up and down.

You – [Indicates identity] Point to the other person.

© William Paul White

Your – [Indicates another person's possession] Push the palm of the *open B hand* toward the other person.

Acknowledgments

You may think that writing a book is a solitary endeavor, but Kathleen's and my experiences with writing *Signs of a Happy Baby* were far different. We couldn't have created this book without our wonderful community.

We'd like to thank all of the families who have learned to sign with their babies in our baby sign language classes over the last ten plus years. We've been touched by so many parents' stories of how baby sign language has helped them build strong family bonds, has created early communication, and has benefitted their whole family.

Kathleen and I would also like to thank the people who supported our baby sign language program from the very beginning: Sheila Dukas Janakos, MPH, Founder of Healthy Horizons; Denise Terry, CEO of EmbraceFamily Health; Angel Ongcapin Barrios, Executive Program Director, Institute for Human and Social Development; and Nancy Held, President and Co-Founder of DayOne Baby.

We have been blessed with the support and teamwork from people at the many locations where we offer our baby sign language program, including Mora Oommen, Executive Director, and Jeanna Lurie, Program Manager, at Blossom Birth Services; E. Kristin Milner Evans, founder and former owner, and Jackie

Velisek, current owner, of Harmony Birth & Family; Scott Brown MPH RD, Health Education Director at Kaiser Permanente, Redwood City; Sharone Mendes Nassi, Founder, Director, and Owner of Carmel Blue, San Francisco; Juliette Espiritu, Support Services Coordinator for the Personal Enrichment Program, Dignity Health Dominican Hospital; Sabrina Freidenfelds, Founder of Then Comes Baby, Oakland; Johnni Parmentier, Health Education Coordinator at Sutter Health, Palo Alto Medical Foundation; Ginny Colbert, Education Director, and Bobbi Williams, Executive Director, at Natural Resources, San Francisco; Pediatrician Tricia Tayama, MD; Kara Karpel, Executive Director, and Julie Dingmann, Infant/Toddler Program Coordinator, CCLC, Families@1st at Cisco; Pat Territo, Director, at Bright Horizons Family Solutions at Letterman Digital Arts Child Care Center; and the many other locations that host our workshops for families.

Thank you to the parents who shared their stories with us, including Sharon, Arie, and Eva Elkins; Aubri, Andrei, Lukas, and Isadora Tallent; Rayna, Toby, Asrai, and Zoe Mayer; Yunting Dai, Philipp Unterbrunner, Elisabeth, and Thomas; Robin, Eric, and Cora Hansen; Colleen, Keith, and Brynn McCallion; Camie, Christian, and Charlie Gadbois; Shannon, Joseph, and Joshua Guzzetta; Samantha Mar; Crystal, Brad, and Emery Christenson; Teri, John, and Robert Voorhes; Miles, Michelle, and Melody Goldstein; Michelle, David, Ethan, and Noah; Caroline Barlerin, Hunter Walk, and Astrid; Carrie, Tal, and Zinnia Shaked; Shawn, Chris, and River Jaquette; Katharina Gleisberg, Arthur and Talea; Chantal Beltran y Puga and Emilia; Julieta Sharma and Victoria; Rick, Sharon, and Charlotte Turlington; Tricia Tayama and Marc; Dori, Jeff and Maddie Gutman; Eugenie and Lilly; Dawn, Barry, and Casey; Steve, Wendy, and Sophie; and the many other families. We loved hearing stories of how signing created more closeness in their families.

Our community includes the dedicated instructors on our team. Instructor Erika Vetter is a force to be reckoned with: a dedicated teacher, smart advisor, and valuable member of our community. We're particularly indebted to Teri Voorhes, who brings grace to all of her sign language classes – and patience and clear-headed calmness to her work as our program manager. Aniko Kovacs generously helps us with our social media. Our team of instructors also includes Cate

Naughton, Courtney Laschkewitsch, Cynthia Phinn, Heidi Locicero, Samantha Garcia, Shirene Massarweh, Thais Skondin, Vanessa Hecht, and Yunting Dai. We'd also like to thank our former instructors Jeff Yao, Erin Carper, Chantal Beltran y Puga, Katharina Gleisberg, Liz Rockstroh, Shannon Jorgensen, Trina Licht, Ana Ayala, Courtney Krueger, Marni Sloves, Annie Morin, Karyn Borella, Laura Keen Server, and Lauren Dugas.

Kathleen and I were blessed to have the help of an amazing crew for the photographing and editing the ASL photographs. Thank you to the one-and-only Lenny Li at lennyliphoto.com for his precise photography work. Sabrina Wong at sabrinawongphoto.com kept us focused and organized during our very long photo-shoot day, and provided post-production and digital artwork on all of the photographs – and we still haven't even scratched the surface of her talents. Courtney Laschkewitsch is a rare find. She brought her ASL knowledge, graphic design skills, and a level of dedication to this project that Kathleen and I will always remember. Unexpected – and welcome – help came from Tamara Macmillan who drove her niece, Jem, to the photo shoot and then stayed to offer all-around production assistance.

Thank you, too, for the patience, flexibility, and vibrant personalities all of our models: Josh Armstrong, Lucia and Ryan Hollowell, Evelyn Hu, Dominique Vincent, and Jem Macmillan (who attended the photo shoot as a makeup artist and graciously stepped in at the last minute to model).

Our models are naturally beautiful/handsome; Rose Hill from makeupcrew.com and her team made them even more so. Thank you to Rose, Lien DeLong, and Jem Macmillan for their hard work during that long day.

My brother, Chris White, is a talented photographer and I'm grateful he could share his talent through the photographs of Kathleen and me.

We're grateful to Angela Lauria and her team at Difference Press for providing everything needed to make this book happen, from the amazing editing skills of Grace Kerina, the design and production expertise of Kelly Pratt and Heidi Miller, and all of the support from the behind-the-scenes team whose work made the process from concept to finished book flow smoothly.

Our family and friends are always there for us, to support us with childcare, carpools, and creative ways to pull Kathleen and me away from our computers.

Thank you to my brother, Chris White; my "other brother," Bob Hortop; my sister, Pamela Truscott-White and my brother-in-law, Ted Truscott; Kathleen's parents, Barbara and Douglas Harper; our nieces and nephews; and Kathleen's wonderfully supportive brothers, sisters, and in-laws – Julia Harper Cooper, Michael and Sally Harper, Laura Harper and Jenn Wright, William and Valerie Harper, and Thomas Harper. It's probably safe to say that we would have rarely left the house to take a break while writing the book if it hadn't been for the planning and gentle prodding from our friends Theresa and James Hackett. In addition, we're grateful for the support we received from Janice Nelson, Christy Miller, Stefanie Soe Benson, Ann Kates, Eliana Armstrong, and Kathryn O'Brien.

Most importantly, Kathleen and I are grateful for our two amazing sons, who inspired our sign language journey and who infuse our lives with love.

About the Authors

Co-authors and co-parents, Kathleen Ann Harper and William Paul White are the couple behind *Signs of a Happy Baby* and an integrated online learning center for parents.

Since 2004, William and his network of instructors have taught fun, interactive, and educational sign language classes and playgroups to more than 13,000 parents. William's brick-and-mortar programs are offered at locations throughout the San Francisco Bay Area, including Kaiser Permanente, Dignity Health, Sutter Health, Blossom Birth, Families@1st at Cisco Systems, and many others. Always fascinated by how people learn, William earned his Bachelor of Science degree from the University of California, Santa Cruz, in psychobiology, the study of behavior from a biological perspective.

Kathleen is a certified life coach and the author of the Amazon bestseller *The Well-Crafted Mom*. In her groups and one-on-one coaching practice, Kathleen integrates coaching support with creative activities to help moms manage the transitions and challenges of motherhood. She holds a Bachelor of Arts degree from San Francisco State University in integrative healing, a specialized major incorporating studies in psychology, philosophy, religion, holistic health, and kinesiology.

Kathleen and William live in the San Francisco Bay Area with their two sons (who both still sign).

Thank You

Keep Signing With Us and Get a Free Introductory Class

Thank you for reading *Signs of a Happy Baby*. We're excited to share our passion for baby sign language – and we're hoping some of it rubbed off on you!

We want baby sign language to become a natural part of your family's everyday routines. Reading about sign language and looking at images is a great start, but we've discovered that the easiest way to learn signs is to see them in action.

To make that happen, we're offering a *free* introductory baby sign language online workshop – a $47 value – to all the readers of our book. The workshop's videos are filled with songs, activities, games, and stories to use when you sign with your baby. They'll help you open a window into your child's world and discover what your baby wants to tell you.

Visit our online learning center at happybabysignsclass.com to enroll in the free class. You'll find everything you need to grow your and your baby's signing skills.

If you have questions, please feel free to ask us. You can send an email to info@signsofahappybaby.com.

Happy signing!
William and Kathleen

Website: happybabysigns.com
Facebook: facebook.com/happybabysigns
Twitter: @HappyBabySigns

Morgan James
Speakers Group

We connect Morgan James published authors with live and online events and audiences who will benefit from their expertise.

Morgan James makes all of our titles available
through the Library for All Charity Organizations.

www.LibraryForAll.org

CPSIA information can be obtained
at www.ICGtesting.com
Printed in the USA
BVHW030609251118
533909BV00005B/28/P

9 781683 502104